Let's Chat

Cultivating Community University Dialogue

A coffee table textbook on partnerships

Let's Chat

Cultivating Community University Dialogue

A coffee table textbook on partnerships

Chapman University | Padres Unidos

Suzanne SooHoo | Patricia Huerta | Patty Perales Huerta-Meza | Tim Bolin | Kevin Stockbridge

Myers
Education
Press

Copyright © 2018 | Myers Education Press, LLC
Published by Myers Education Press, LLC
P.O. Box 424 Gorham, ME 04038

Library of Congress Cataloging-in-Publication Data available from Library of Congress.

13-digit ISBN 978-1-9755-0040-5 (paperback)
13-digit ISBN 978-1-9755-0039-9 (hard cover)
13-digit ISBN 978-1-9755-0041-2 (library networkable e-edition)
13-digit ISBN 978-1-9755-0042-9 (consumer e-edition)

Printed in the United States of America.
All first editions printed on acid-free paper that meets the American National Standards Institute Z39-48 standard.

Books published by Myers Education Press may be purchased at special quantity discount rates for groups, workshops, training organizations and classroom usage. Please call our customer service department at 1-800-232-0223 for details.

Cover and book design by the SooHoo creative team.

Visit us on the web at www.myersedpress.com to browse our complete list of titles.

Table of Contents

Acknowledgements

We wish to express our deep appreciation to:

God Almighty, whomever that may be in your life, for giving us the strength, knowledge, ability, and opportunity to undertake this book project and speak together of our community experience.

All Padres Unidos families whose life stories, personal journeys, courage, and strength have made this book come to life in a vulnerable and authentic way.

Padres Unidos board members whose collaboration made the gift of this book possible. Special recognition goes to Judith Magsaysay whose insight and leadership led to the mutual introduction of Chapman University and Padres Unidos as partners.

Paulo Freire Democratic Project: Peter McLaren, Anaida Colon-Muniz, Lilia Monzo, Miguel Zavala, Cathery Yeh, Jorge Rodriguez, Gerry McNenny, and particularly cofounders Tom Wilson and

Suzanne SooHoo, whose collective inspiration and work prepared Chapman researchers to imagine more equitable and democratic approaches in partnerships.

Chapman colleagues: President Daniele Struppa, Dean Margaret Grogan, former Dean Don Cardinal, Anat Herzog, and Quaylan Allen for their support of this partnership and initiative. Special thank you to Charlotte Evensen for assembling our scope and sequence.

Chris Myers and the Myers Education Press team who stepped out with us in the creation of a new genre and tirelessly worked to make this book possible.

Elders, storytellers, and mentors who paved the way to prepare each of our hearts and minds for a wealth of wisdom and openness that lead to this partnership.

Introduction

Chapman University and Padres Unidos

Chapman University is a comprehensive university located in Orange, California. Members of the writing team for this book come from Padres Unidos, a nonprofit organization and the Paulo Freire Democratic Project (PFDP), which is housed in the Attallah College of Educational Studies. The scholarship, teaching, and service within the PFDP are heavily influenced by the philosophy and work of Brazilian educator, Paulo Freire.

Padres Unidos is a grassroots community organization devoted to parent education and school readiness, primarily serving Latino families located in Santa Ana, California. They refer to themselves as community workers who believe successful families build successful communities. They have educated over 34,000 parents and children in the past decade.

In 2010, a local educator, Judy Magsaysay, brought Padres Unidos and Chapman's Freirean educators together because she recognized Freirean values in their respective missions and programs and speculated a possible partnership. Padres' goals were to affirm its program and organic curriculum through university certification; to create organizational allies within the community; and to bring the university into the community's psyche as a resource for the families. Freirean researchers were interested in exploring the Freirean connection; in bridging community wisdom with academic theory; in connecting theory to people's lived experiences and problems; and in implementing culturally responsive (Berryman, SooHoo, & Nevin, 2013) and ethically sound ways of working with communities, essentially by working *with* and not *on* them.

Latinos living in the same community walked around the campus for years without ever recognizing it as a place where they might belong. We lived parallel lives in the same sandbox and seldom turned toward each other, except to occasionally throw sand at one another. Making a departure from this code, the Padres-Chapman partnership aimed to build a deeper and more meaningful relationship than simple co-existence. We chose to build a long-term relationship where we created multiple pathways of intersections between our neighbors and the university, as well as ways to see each other in our futures.

Implicit in Padres Unidos' conditions for a partnership is a disruption of traditional power relationships between universities and communities. Historically, universities provide experts to the community and a power relationship is understood with the ivory tower weighing in as a heavyweight and the community as a featherweight (Saltmarsh & Hartley, 2011). Padres Unidos' invitation to engage called for a respect of boundaries with inferred parity of power.

In other words, they were aware of the inclination of universities to exert uninvited dominance over a partnership relationship and, therefore, they proposed the conditions of collaboration up front in an authentic and transparent way. The challenge to us at the university was, would we accept this invitation to participate under these conditions, unarmed with conventional privileged credentials but bringing with us an eagerness to learn and a willingness to earn increasing credibility over time? (SooHoo & Huerta, 2017).

Not only did Padres Unidos motivate university researchers to act differently from the typical community service orientation where university experts deposit knowledge into the community, Padres Unidos was offering an opportunity to craft a relationship based on mutual respect for different knowledge systems, where university knowledge and local knowledge were equally valued. From beyond, our muse and community patron saint, Paulo Freire, reminded us:

> *[Those] who come from 'another world' to the world of people who do so not as invaders.*
> *They do not come to teach or to transmit or to give anything, but rather to learn, with the people,*
> *about the people's world. (Freire, 1998, p. 180)*

Learning How to be in Partnership

This book is about learning how to be in the relationship called a community university partnership. It is about:

- learning how to relate with one another in a long-term relationship
- learning to work with each other without trying to change each other
- learning to respect each other's knowledge systems and epistemologies
- learning to listen and work with each other's incompleteness
- learning to co-create and evolve with each other
- learning to live democratically to facilitate each other's full and equal participation

Let's Chat serves as a capstone to our literacy project of mutual learning and knowledge generation, and it hopes to capture the voices and the soul of the community and university members. Our intention is to put forward ideas in straightforward and powerful ways so that students, academics and community members can understand how to map community university relationships, with the goal of improving the overall health of our communities. We also wanted a book that will be read by the hundreds of immigrant families that have effected or have been affected by Padres Unidos – a book they can identify with, one that represents their personal and collective journeys toward self-empowerment. As they join with university partners in the cocreation of this book, we present what we have learned together.

A New Genre: A Coffee Table Textbook

Coming from the home of the Paulo Freire Democratic Project at Chapman University and nonprofit community organization Padres Unidos, the Chapman University Padres Unidos Partnership offers this, a coffee table textbook, *Let's Chat: Cultivating Community University Dialogue*. The book presents a collection of community stories, research memos, reflections, and analysis that highlight the journey of border crossings between two coexisting neighbors: the community and the university. It brings light to the differences between the two cultures and the socially constructed divide that maintains that separation. Stories from the faculty and community members represent how they disrupted the barriers that typically divide us through the formation of a partnership. By reconceptualizing how universities and communities can work together to reshape the intellectual landscape and reconfigure power differentials, this book serves as a powerful model for how to be in relationship within community–university partnerships. Using accessible language, it illustrates the elements of a successful relationship and emphasizes resistance to the division between academic knowledge and local knowledge. Written *with* and *by* the community, this collection amplifies the voices of immigrant families, community-based researchers, doctoral research assistants, and other community stake holders. Inspired by these voices, we hope that readers will be motivated to engage individually and collectively with the end-of-chapter reflections called *Cafecitos*. We use this word to suggest a way to engage and enjoy this book. We suggest sitting with someone from the community or university, accompanied by your favorite beverage, and deeply engaging in meaningful conversations about the stories and concepts in this book. As contributors, we hope to inspire courage and creativity to build relational bridges between two sectors in society as we collectively remap the community university intellectual landscape.

Coffee table books are usually non-fiction books filled with pictures that inspire conversation. They are typically a light read and therefore relatively uninhabited by jargon to allow for casual perusal. We hope this textbook with coffee table appeal will be attractive to:

– university students in service learning/civic engagement programs
– nonprofit community organizations, community stakeholders, and immigrant families
– professors and partnerships engaged in partnership work or community-based research
– school districts interested in parent engagement programs
– professional organizations focused on community engagement

There has been a growing interest across the nation in community-based research, civic engagement, and community–university partnerships. In California in particular, school districts under parent engagement Local Control and Accountability Plans (LCAP) legislation have explored and experimented with various forms of parent engagement and school-community collaborations. Given the current political emphasis on school choice, vouchers, and charters, policymakers, community stakeholders, and media have placed a bright spotlight on the relationships between communities and learning institutions.

Keeping multiple audiences in mind, *Let's Chat* was carefully designed to be:

– accessible and conversational
– interactive and conceptually engaging
– a textbook that is compelling to read with short chapters, lessons, and activities
– aesthetically pleasing
– a tool for uniting academic and community wisdom

Accessibility

Responding to the American Educational Research Association's (AERA) call for action, asking academics and intellectuals to communicate to policymakers and the public in accessible language, our goal is to deconstruct the artificial divide between "academic-speak" and "community speak." bell hooks (2004) affirms this direction when she urges us "to speak simply with language that is accessible to as many folks as possible… (T)he use of language and style of presentation that alienates most folks who are not academically trained reinforces the notion that the academic world is separate from real life… It is a false dichotomy" (p. 26).

Many publications that come out of community university partnerships are written in academic-ese. They were written for a tenure file rather than for an audience of community members or college freshmen in community engagement programs. Seldom are they co-authored by scholars and local folks.

Language used in this coffee table textbook was constructed to be conversational. Two sets of questions punctuate each chapter to engage the reader with thoughtful reflection, either individually or with a Cafecito partner in dialogue. The style of presentation is enhanced for accessibility by graphic representations to illustrate the opening story and concept of each chapter. Graphics as a third language to community voices and academic speak is like an accompanying hula, where graceful hands interpret songs. Graphics bring evocative imagery to help to imprint the stories in our minds. They are both the beginning and the lingering scent of each chapter.

Conversations and Community Engagement

Conversations and dialogue have the potential to bring people together to enact social change. Studies (Brown & Issacs, 2005; Wheatley, 2009) show that conversations are ideal conditions for change. Conversations are places for us to worry and dream together. Members of our partnership testify that it was in conversations and dialogue that transformation occurred both individually and collectively. In learning to work together, dialogue in cultural circles were the spiritual lassos that bounded our combined histories to face new future possibilities. We hope this book will be used to cultivate the art of conversation between universities and communities. We invite readers to read the book *in community* and start community-based conversations.

Format of the Book

People of different backgrounds and interests can take different things from this book. Some folks may be interested in the community's stories that Santa Ana parents have used when raising their children. Some people may solely be interested in the partnership concepts and therefore focus on each story's *Discussion*. Others may be interested in relationship building by engaging in cross-sectional conversations and dialogues through the *Cafecitos*. And finally, some individuals may prefer to engage in the community/civic engagement curriculum and therefore will participate in the *Activities*.

For college instructors, we have provided a scope and sequence at the end of the book in the appendix. This chart strings together reflective questions and community/university activities from each chapter. The mini-chapters are ideal for 50-minute period class sessions and lesson starters. Reports show that students have received little to no training before going out to community engagement or service learning activities. This book, with its combined wisdom of community and university, may prove useful before and during a community-based initiative.

The book is organized into three sections: Coming to Know (teal – the encounter), Becoming (red – learning), and Belonging (purple – philosophy). However, you can enter this book at any place and find something meaningful, based on the readers' need. Our coffee table book makes a constructivist assumption – that is, the reader may choose to synthesize various chapters without depending on the linearity of a continuous story line. Consequently, the reading of this book is reader-directed, based on need and interest, and chapters can be read in any order.

We hope you enjoy this book, but most importantly, we hope some good conversations and meaningful insights come from it.

References

Brown, J. & Issacs, D. (2005). *The World Café: Shaping our futures through conversations that matter.* San Francisco, Ca: Berrett-Koehler.

Freire, P. (2010). *Pedagogy of the oppressed.* NY: Continuum International Publishing Group.

hooks, b. (2004). Keeping Close to Home: Class and Education. In Muth, M. (Ed.), *Community voices: academic, work, and public readings.* NY: Pearson 22 — 32.

Saltmarsh, J., & Hartley, M. (2011). *"To serve a larger purpose": Engagement for democracy and the transformation of higher education.* Temple University Press: Philadelphia, PA.

SooHoo, S. & Huerta, P. (2017). At the partnership table: Bridging academia and community through horizontal dialoguing. In Carty, V. & Luevano, R. (Eds.), *Mobilizing Public Sociology.* Leiden, The Netherlands: Brill.

Wheatley, M.J. (2009). *Turning to one another: Simple conversations to restore hope to the future* (2nd ed). San Francisco, CA: Berrett-Koehler.

Section 1: Coming to Know

Imagine the university and the community as two toddlers playing at opposite ends of a sandbox. Using Roland S. Barth's (2006) famous metaphor of parallel play, both are so engrossed in their own work that they seldom interact with each other except for inadvertently throwing sand in the other's face. What does it take for these two to turn towards each other? To build a sandcastle?

The centrality of relationships is often secondary in forming mergers or partnerships. In this partnership, relationships inform who we are and how we are with each other. As social justice workers, we find that our primary vocation is to create environments where human beings can be more human. Grace Lee Boggs cites Martin Luther King's definition of love as a willingness to go to any lengths to restore or create such communities. Our work is about people, with people, for people. Furthermore, she urges us to come to know people with our hearts and not only with our eyes (Boggs, 2011). The primacy of developing and sustaining relationships are consequently awarded the highest priority in our community university encounter accompanied by our underlying respect and reverence for each other.

The partnership was formed over a lunch meeting with various community representatives and two faculty members from the Paulo Freire Democratic Project. This ritual of breaking bread soon marked every subsequent meeting and facilitated a culinary way of coming to know each other. While food was a familiar way to explore coming to know people, hugging was relatively unfamiliar in professional context for university partners. Hugs for greetings, allyship, comfort, and healing were integral to Padres Unidos and soon became a comfortable ritual of encounter.

Here are the initial questions we had for each other. What new protocols, norms, forms of knowledge and new epistemological landscapes might we explore together? What opportunities could we discover to build bridges between these two sectors? Why do we need each other? What is the university's capacity for connectedness? (Palmer, 2004). What does it take to prepare ourselves to be "in partnership" together?

The chapters in Section 1 are marked in bold. The three mini-chapters describe the history of demarcation between university scholars and community members. We talk about the juxtaposition of **Knowledge**, both practical knowledge and theoretical knowledge. We question how researchers who typically see the world through questions, data and scientific analysis reconcile their work with concerned and passionate community groups who are interested in creating a change (Muth, 2004). Because some community members hold no degrees, and their ideas are not supported by data, their knowledge is largely ignored (Gies, 2017).

Togethering describes our ways of getting to know each other and feeling comfortable in each other's workplace environments, how food was necessary accompaniment to conversations, dialogue, and storytelling (SooHoo & Huerta, 2017). What we didn't know in the beginning was how fundamental Togethering would be in developing, maintaining, and sustaining our partnership.

A **Partnership** is born to learn how to be in relationship with each other — the community eager to be validated for the ways they have strengthened their communities. And the university's pledge, to work with the community, for the community, as judged by community standards.

References

Barth, R. S. (2006). Improving relationships within the schoolhouse. *Educational Leadership, 62*(6), 8-13.

Boggs, G. L. (2011). *The next American revolution.* Berkeley, CA: University of California Press.

Gies, E. (2017). The meaning of lichen: How a self-taught naturalist unearthed hidden symbioses in the wilds of british columbia - and helped to overturn 150 years of accepted scientific wisdom. *Scientific American,* 53-59. http://ericagies.com/write/the-meaning-of-lichen-scientific-american/

Muth, M. (2004). *Community voices: Academic, work, and public readings.* New York, NY: Pearson.

Palmer, P. (2004). The quest for community in higher education. In M. Muth (Ed.), *Community voices: Academic, work, and public readings.* New York, NY: Pearson 33 — 42.

SooHoo, S., & Huerta, P. (2017). At the partnership table: Bridging academia and community through horizontal dialoguing. In V. Carty & R. Luevano (Eds.), *Mobilizing public sociology.* Leiden, The Netherlands: Brill.

PARTNERSHIP

Story: Tamales

Early one morning, a knock on the front door was heard in Ana's house. She ignored the sound. Ana was trying to sleep in because it was school vacation. But her mom called to her, "Open the door, Ana! Welcome the people in." Reluctantly, Ana got up and did as her mom said. At the door stood neighbors with arms full of food and smiles on their faces. "We came to help make tamales!" In no time, they had made their way into the kitchen. Everyone's face was bright, except Ana's, who made it clear that she just wanted to be left alone.

Grumpily, Ana locked herself in her bedroom. The noise level in the house got louder and louder as even more people came to prepare Christmas tamales. She wasn't happy to have all the noise. Eventually, she heard a knock on her bedroom door and the voice of her mother saying, "Come out and join us, Ana!"

Ana walked into the kitchen with her mother. It was filled with family and neighbors, all singing and laughing. The air was filled with sweet and savory smells. Ana was trying hard to remain grumpy in the midst of all this merriment. When her mother turned to her and said, "Don't be so negative, *mija!* It's tamale-making day!," Ana replied, "Why can't we just do it alone?" Her mom laughed, "No one makes tamales alone. It takes a community! All these people have come to share this time with us. It's the coming together of many hands and hearts that makes tamales so good!"

Finally, Ana smiled. She knew her mom was right. Tamale-making day was the best day of the year because it brought all the people she loved together. She turned to her mom and asked, "How can I help?" Soon she was up to her elbows in maza.

LET'S CHAT
CAFECITO I (Individual or Dialogue)

What events include the gathering of your family and friends? Are there traditions, like tamale making, that are centered around working together?

Can you name something in life that would be impossible to do without the assistance of colleagues, friends, strangers, or family?

Did you ever resist the help of others only to later realize that you needed them?

Discussion

Historically, the common interest of communities and universities had been upset by the physical and ideological severing of relations. Physically, Hall (2015) traces the dissolution of the community and university relationship to the enclosure movement of the 12th century, when large tracks of collectively farmed land were distributed to individual landowners. The University of Cambridge was founded during the enclosure movement, which had the effect of creating a division between academic and common knowledge (Hall, 2015). The division of university and community physical space lends to the creation of differentiated value, where university knowledge was more valuable than the community's. Bookchin (2005) posited that there was a "spirit of cooperation within the community itself, and between community and nature," which was disrupted as the communal relationships dissolved (p. 416). Since the time of the break-up of the community, idealists, politicians, and academics have endeavored to resolve the problem by seeking mutual benefits.

Best practice regarding community and university relationships is often couched in terms of mutual benefits (Davis, 2013). However, in reality, even these goals are rarely realized and have even been exploited (Saltmarsh & Hartley, 2011). Contemporary analysts note that a significant obstacle to partnerships is the reframing of education as a private benefit rather than a "value in-itself" (Maurrasse, 2001); in student populations (Saltmarsh & Hartley, 2011); for faculty members (Brinkley-Rubinstein & McGuire, 2016); and in university policy (Vasilache, Dima, & Dan, 2011). As a consequence, contemporary analysts note that community and university partnerships have lost their communal, largely democratic interests.

However, there are programs that have successfully implemented many of the best practices. In a nationally recognized university and community partnership program at Vanderbilt University, the department of Human and Organizational Development (HOD) was built upon the values of mutual interest, shared democratic values, and active engagement (Brinkley-Rubinstein & McGuire, 2016). At Miami University's Center for Community Engagement (CCE), campus and community are brought together in various configurations in what they describe as meaning-making conversation, reflection, and *sometimes action* (Morton & Bergbauer, 2015). Brinkley-Rubinstein and McGuire (2016) agreed that for relationships to be sustainable and mutually beneficial, there needs to be a shared appreciation of the importance of the partner's knowledge. "To develop authentic partnerships instead of university-directed agreements is rooted in the notion that university programs and university researchers need to learn as much from the school and community as the school and the community need to learn from the university" (Grogan & Fahrenwald, 2017, p. 1).

Both institutions view the community as a rich learning opportunity, joining universities across the United States in developing or enacting a form of civic engagement through the creation of community collaborations. Note that Miami University's *sometimes action* means that creating relationships are paramount in their collaborations, reflecting the goals to create new identities, knowledge and communities together. Pasifika and Maori worked across university-community boundaries to develop new hybrid research and collective identities (Cave, Johnston, Morrison, & Underhill-Sem, 2012). They constructed an "organic melding of identities that, without losing individual uniqueness, retains and fosters the unity" (Bookchin, 2005, p. 118).

Feminist researchers summarize how our ideologies might shift in partnerships as they argue for "collapsing of the social hierarchies that elevate the academy over the community, the office/laboratory over the field site, the researcher over the researched, and the institutionalization of knowledge in the global north over the generation of knowledge in the global south" (Wright, 2008, p. 381).

The dissolution of the divide between communities and universities paves the way for the reconciliation of the scholarly activist (university researcher who works on behalf of community) and organic intellectual (community member who speaks on behalf of the community). By shrinking the hierarchy created when the community was cut out of academic affairs, the community member is freed to participate in academic spaces. Furthermore, scholarly activists would have the potential to become organic intellectuals, becoming indistinguishable from the communities in which they are located.

LET'S CHAT
CAFECITO II (Individual or Dialogue)

What questions or actions would you consider when developing an action plan for community engagement?

Who would you talk to before implementing your plan in the community? At the university?

Activity

Craft a step-by-step plan on how you would build relationships with those whom you wish to engage. Include community protocols you would observe. Working on the tenet of relationships first, describe the relationship-building activities you would engage in and assess the vitality of the relationship before launching an initiative. Make a list of the community leaders (organic intellectuals) who might share community stories with you.

References

Bookchin, M. (2005). *The ecology of freedom: The emergence and dissolution of hierarchy.* Oakland, CA: AK Press.

Brinkley-Rubinstein, L., & McGuire, A. (2016). *Academics in action!: A model for community-engaged research, teaching, and service.* New York, NY: Fordham University Press.

Cave, J., Johnston, L., Morrison, C., & Underhill-Sem, Y. (2012). Community-university collaborations: Creating hybrid research and collective identities. *Kōtuitui: New Zealand Journal of Social Sciences Online, 7*(1), 37-50.

Davis, K. (2013). University and community partnerships: Building successful and mutually beneficial relationships while addressing university readiness and the unequal balance of power. https://www.ohio.edu/education/centers-and-partnerships/centers/center-for-higher-education/news.cfm

Grogan, M., & Fahrenwald, C. (2017). *Networks between universities and community organizations in teacher education.* Chapman University & University of Upper Austria. Unpublished manuscript.

Hall, B. L. (2015). *Beyond epistemicide: Knowledge democracy and higher education.* Paper presented at the International Symposium on Higher Education in the Age of Neo Liberalism and Audit Cultures, University of Regina.

Maurrasse, D. J. (2001). *Beyond the campus: How colleges and universities form partnerships with their communities.* New York, NY: Routledge.

Morton, K., & Bergbauer, S. (2015). A case for community: Starting with relationships and prioritizing community as method in service-learning. *Michigan Journal of Community Service Learning, Fall,* 18-31.

Saltmarsh, J., & Hartley, M. (2011). *"To serve a larger purpose": Engagement for democracy and the transformation of higher education.* Temple University Press: Philadelphia, PA.

Vasilache, S., Dima, A. M., & Dan, M. (2011). The relationship between university research and the marketability of universities. *Amfiteatru Economic, 13*(30), 544-554.

Wright, M. (2008). Gender and geography: Knowledge and activism across the intimately global. *Progress in Human Geography, 33*(3), 379-386.

TOGETHERING

Story: Making Community

It's a typical Monday morning in this modest home in Santa Ana, California. The house is full of Latinas busy with activities: some at table meetings, some organizing boxes of teaching materials, and others preparing food in the kitchen. The dining room table doubles as the operational hub for Padres Unidos The copy machine is humming in the background. Telephones are in constant use. Ladies take turns noting information on a wall-sized whiteboard in the dining room.

On this morning, a handful of university researchers can be heard knocking. They have come to participate in a weekly meeting of the organization's parent educators. When the door opens, virtually every person in the house greets them with a long hug. The embrace is accompanied by, "¡Hola! ¡Buenos dias! ¿Como estas?"

The bustle of the house focuses on preparing the meeting. Boxes of sweet and savory treats, platters of pan dulce, and an array of fruit all appear in the center of the large living room. The smell of coffee brewing from the kitchen competes with the zesty aroma of pozole simmering in a big cauldron. People get their food and settle into the sofas and folding chairs arranged in a large circle. Someone says a prayer to bless the food and all who have come.

In the meeting, Padres Unidos' educators share stories in Spanish of the week's activities at their schools. They pose problems and a circle dialogue ensues. They offer each other solutions couched in stories. Sometimes they enact or dramatize a solution. These women are spin-masters, offering wisdom and experiences about new issues. All the while, the researchers are listening as a translator assists them. All have come to this place as listeners and participants. Every moment, every act, and every space facilitate togethering.

LET'S CHAT
CAFECITO I (Individual or Dialogue)

What are some of the customary practices in your community when you gather together?

Hugging is a big part of greeting newcomers in this story. How does your community welcome somebody new?

If hugging was uncomfortable for you as a newcomer, what would you say or do? How could you let others know?

Discussion

> *"I learned how to hug my teenage son. I learned how to hug my husband."*
> *(Padres Unidos graduation speech)*

One might not expect to hear these words at a graduation ceremony at a youth correctional facility. After a six-month program from Padres Unidos, parents with youth in juvenile hall and probation come together to celebrate their growth and accomplishment. As words above darted through the assembly hall, they triggered tears and sniffles from those in attendance. This included fellow graduates, incarcerated youth, probationary guards, distinguished guests from the Archdiocese, police officers, and Chapman University representatives. We all silently recognized how life's challenges can easily cause us to lose our humanity, to suppress a hug, and to withdraw from personal intimacy.

Relearning to hug a family member who has been incarcerated comes with new-found forgiveness and self-reflective recovery from guilt and shame at having lost that instinct. For some, we never learned the art of hugging and therefore, may be uncomfortable in this foreign physical space. Hugging involves reciprocal physicality: giving a hug and being hugged. Embodied knowing is integral to togethering. As Antonia Darder (2014) reminds us, the physical self is inextricable from the human experience. Hugging is an expression of human feeling and "a commitment to counter the disembodiment of our humanity" (p. 70).

For Padres Unidos, when one person hugs another, they share a common heartbeat. Hugs console. They show affection and solidarity. In this organization, hugs also act as healing therapy during emotionally stressful times, such as recounting child abuse, domestic abuse, poverty, and/or immigration problems. There is a common Maori tradition in New Zealand that is, like hugging, an embodied way to come to know another. When Maori meet someone new for the first time in a formal setting, a handshake is accompanied by a nose-to-nose exchange (hongi), which results inevitably in face-to-face contact. This exchange allows one to look into the soul of the other and to share a common breath of friendship. No matter the practice, human connection and physical bonding cultivate togethering, group trust, and human kinship.

The space created by a hug is a sacred space. It may be described as liminal space, or the in-between. It is a place of potentiality, where transformation may occur as two realities/persons are actively pulled into relationship (McLaren, 2000). Liminal spaces can be transformative because they are not subject to one perspective or another, but exist in the tension between both. Such spaces are similar to Bhahba's third space, which suggested "continuous intermingling and flowing back and forth between the two spaces... not a totally separate sphere, but one that embraces both sides" (English, 2002, p. 110). The act of togethering explores the geography of the liminal space together.

The world is not held together by molecules but by stories. (Author Unknown)

The language of our partnership is punctuated by stories. "We tell stories because that is the way of our culture," noted a Padres parent. These stories are subjective accounts and reckonings of life. Hearing them led Chapman partners to recognize that their conventional training as researchers sought to sterilize work in the field. Normative academic measures tend to prioritize objective knowledge over subjectivity for fear of bias. Such approaches nullify the richness and intent of stories. Therefore, researchers needed to learn a new stance as partners by participating in the language of storytelling.

Frank (2010), a sociologist, invites us to ask questions such as: What do stories do to inform human life? What are their functions? Stories deal with human troubles, display human character, purport a point of view, direct us, heal us, mobilize social movements, convey morality, move us away from trouble, resonate with other people's experiences, tell truths, and arouse imagination, suspense and compassion. Stories are performances that are adjusted to fit multiple circumstances (Frank, 2010). They are ways of capturing the complex meanings of one's lived reality in forms that are comprehensible to others (Stockbridge, 2015). Furthermore, stories are where each voice is heard. They transform the teller and the listener (SooHoo, 2006). Stories tell of and enact togethering.

"I must eat or I will die" (Lupita, 7 years old)

These are the words of a seven-year-old sister of a recently incarcerated youth. She explained that her parents were struggling financially due to the many costs incurred in having a detained youth. She ran, dragging the youth educator by the hand toward the front door of juvenile hall with a huge smile on her face. "Tuesdays are my favorite! I love coming here! I feel so loved! I get to talk about what makes me happy, mad or sad. I get lots of hugs but the bestest, my most favorite thing, is that we get pizza!" Food is a universal and necessary act. It has long assumed a role in our society beyond filling empty stomachs — it permeates many facets of our life. For Lupita, the pizza was a welcomed treat that brought many sensory enjoyments at physiological, psychological and social levels.

Urie Bronfenbrenner, architect of ecological psychology, provided a powerful platform for understanding human relationships and the role of bio-psycho-social factors (Bronfenbrenner, 1977, 1979). Since the introduction of his ecological theory, people have begun to look at human development and relationships beyond the static characteristics of traits and abilities within individuals. Such a stance views behavior and learning in relation to the dynamic interplay between the biological, psychological, social, and historical contexts in which they occur. This can include realities such as food and meals.

For the partnership, food has been present at every event. Transcending physical nourishment, food acts as a bridge to holistic connectedness. Recently a study in the *Journal of Psychological Science* concluded that turning to comfort foods can improve a person's mood and positive cognitions. Data from this research showed a decrease in feelings of loneliness and improvements in an overall sense of well-being when food associated with warm feelings and good thoughts were consumed (Gómez-Pinilla, 2008). In the partnership, the food brought to the table is no longer just food. It is a way of extending oneself for the growth and well-being of the other. It is a way of togethering. We bring food that we know other attendees will enjoy. Our foods acknowledge our cultural diversity and seek inclusion. The partners no longer view the relationship through their own lens, but carry the "other" within.

As a result of Padres Unidos' and Chapman University members' collaborative efforts toward togethering, we were able to start the process of understanding each other better. We started by rethinking ways of communication and reprioritizing embodied knowledge within a fuller language system. We have grown though sharing space, by eating meals together and through hugs. Together we hoped to realize our mutual goal of a deeper sense of partnership, transcending normative academic ways of knowing.

LET'S CHAT
CAFECITO II (Individual or Dialogue)

What does togethering look like for you? What does it sound like? What does it smell and taste like?

What is the feeling of togethering? How can you bring this into an organization or a partnership?

Activity

Set up a time to have a shared meal with other people that you would like to come to know. As you prepare for the meal, consider talking about the ways that certain foods, spaces, conversations, and rituals of greetings allow for and/or hinder the practice of togethering.

References

Bronfenbrenner, U. (1977). Toward an experimental ecology of human development. *American Psychologist*, 32, 513-531.

Bronfenbrenner, U. (1979). *The ecology of human development. Experiments by nature and design.* Cambridge, Massachusetts: Harvard University Press.

Darder, A. (2014). *Freire and education.* New York, NY: Routledge.

English, L. (2002). *Third space: Contested space, identity and international adult education.* Paper presented at the CASAE/ACEEA 21 Annual conference: Adult Education and the contested terrain of public policy, Toronto, Canada.

Frank, A.W. (2010) *Letting stories breath: a socio-narratology.* Chicago: University of Chicago Press.

Gómez-Pinilla, F. (2008). Brain foods: The effects of nutrients on brain functioning. *Nature Reviews Neuroscience*, 9, 568-578.

McLaren, P. (2000). *Che Guevara, Paulo Freire, and the pedagogy of revolution*: Rowman & Littlefield Publishers.

SooHoo, S. (2006). *Talking leaves.* Cresskill, NJ: Hampton Press.

Stockbridge, K. (2015). A critical resurrection: breathing the spirit into an education of despair. In C. Achieng-Evensen, J. Dimick, N. Kitonga, M. Krikorian, K. Stockbridge & B. Kanpol. *The critical graduate experience: An ethics of higher education responsibilities.* (pp. 23-38). NewYork: Lang.

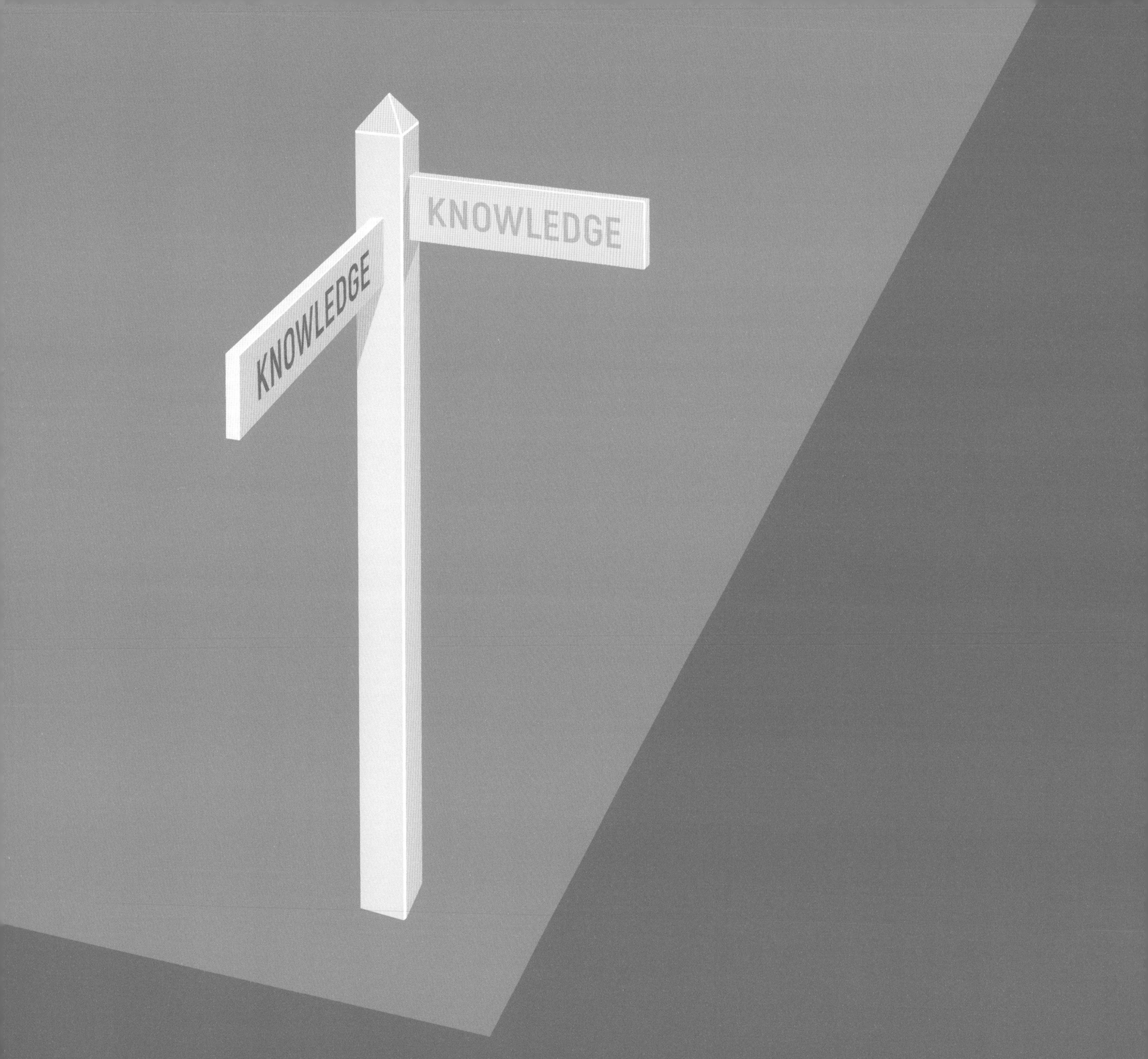
KNOWLEDGE
KNOWLEDGE

Story: The Bus Into the City

One day, a little country mouse decided to take a trip to the big city. He had never been out of the country before! When the city bus pulled up, he joined a group of city mice. As the bus made its way into town, all the mice enjoyed the ride.

When the bus reached the city, it made its regular stop at a restaurant. All the other mice went into the restaurant to enjoy whatever meal they chose to eat. However, this was the little country mouse's first time in a restaurant. He had never seen so much food! He didn't know what to eat. He smelled the delicious chorizo and thought he would eat that. But as he was about to choose the chorizo, he smelled some amazing bread. He changed his mind and started to choose that instead. But then other items intrigued him. There were so many choices, he wasn't able to decide what he should eat.

Soon, he heard all the other mice saying, "Let's go! Let's go! Let's go!" The bus was getting ready to leave and they needed to make sure that they weren't left behind. So the little country mouse ran back onto the bus with all the others. He didn't even have anything to eat at the restaurant! Together the mice rode back into the country.

Upon getting home, the mice jumped off the bus and began to chat about all the things they had eaten. They really enjoyed their trip! But the little country mouse said, "I don't like the city." The others asked him, "Why?" He replied, "Because you cannot make up your mind what you want to eat, and then they take you away and you are left hungry."

LET'S CHAT
CAFECITO I (Individual or Dialogue)

How do you imagine the story would read if there were a city mouse taking his first bus trip into the country? What challenges would the city mouse encounter?

What knowledge do you bring to the conversation from your family and homes (funds of knowledge)? How is that knowledge the same or different from the knowledge that you have at school or at work?

Discussion

This story provides an example of unequal knowledge. There are city mice who *know* and a country mouse who does *not know* how to eat at restaurants, resulting in superiority of one kind of knowledge over another. In fact, knowing what to do was the difference between eating and going hungry. The country mouse was not inherently unintelligent, but lacked valuable knowledge for this situation. We might imagine that a city mouse might be lacking valued knowledge if he were to find himself thrown into the country.

The way that people come to know the world is called their epistemology. It is connected to their culture. Culture is a fluid space of practices influenced by shared knowledges, values, beliefs, language, and ways of making meaning. Epistemology is "where our thoughts take shape" (Kirkland, 2015, p. 183). Culturally, people share common meanings of knowledge as well as shared ways of expressing knowledge through actions and emotions. Communities and universities each have their own cultures of knowing.

Institutions of education have a cultural history of creating knowledge ladders or epistemological hierarchies. They have ranked knowledge systems against each other, valuing certain ways of knowing more than others. Hall (2015) suggests that "the act of creating Oxford and the other medieval universities was an act of enclosing knowledge, limiting access to knowledge, exerting a form of control over knowledge and providing a means for a small elite to acquire this knowledge for purposes of leadership" (p. 2). The consolidation of knowledge in universities had the further effect of creating two classes of knowledge, those within the institutions ("knowers") and those out in the community ("non-knowers") (Hall, 2015, p. 2). The physical separation of these groups by university walls served to assert that possessing right knowledge moved one into a higher status.

To this day, epistemological differentiation has created a false sense of superiority. Shor and Freire (1987) observed that knowledge which is created within universities is given more value than outside knowledge. Moreover, universities are perceived as knowledge generators and communities as knowledge consumers (Sullivan, 2000). By not acknowledging the community's inherent knowledge capital, or "funds of knowledge" (Moll, Amanti, Neff, & Gonzalez, 1992), universities risk the starvation and ultimate death of community knowledge. This would mean epistemicide or epistemological nihilation (King, 2017). Unfed and malnourished, due to the dominance of the academy, community and indigenous identities, and their accompanying wisdoms, may fade from relevancy.

Some in higher education are taking note of this separation. In well-intentioned efforts to bridge the divide between commoners and the educated elite, universities typically approach community partners believing themselves to be saviors. Many of those universities also believe that they have solutions to impart rather than seeing themselves as equals (Saltmarsh & Hartley, 2011). Instead of coupling knowledge systems, well-meaning university "experts" have dominated their community partners. Some community organizations may acquiesce to this, recognizing that they could gain greater status in partnership with a university. However, members of these organizations are often left feeling pitied or forced into compromise as a result.

In our partnership, we wondered in what ways knowledge could be equitably shared, honored, and made to be mutually beneficial. The notion of multilogicality (Berryman, SooHoo, & Nevin, 2013; Cormier, 2011; Kincheloe, 2008) assists us in sustaining the integrity of various epistemologies. Multilogicality comes out of the field of quantum physics where scientists have demonstrated that light can be simultaneously a particle and a wave. It contends that diversity of thought need not be resolved through assimilation. Community and university partners can maintain their ways of knowing as valued equals. As a result, Padres Unidos, in partnership with a university, is provided academic legitimacy without requiring them to compromise the community wisdom that made them so successful.

What allows a partnership to flower as a space of equity? It requires recognizing the ways that power is at play in the different values that are given to knowledge systems. Critical educators argue that university researchers should ask themselves questions such as, "What knowledge?" "Whose knowledge?" "Who benefits?" and "Whose interests are being served and at what price?" (Barlow & Robertson, 1994; Boyles, 1998; Fabos and Young, 1999; Young, 1994 & Fernández-Balboa, 1993 as cited by White, Cooper, & Mackey, 2014, p. 133). Skepticism of academic knowledge and its complicity with inequality fueled our commitment to avert epistemological domination. By keeping these and similar questions as open topics of discussion in our partnership, we challenge the unequal value of privileged knowledge and structures of exclusion.

A salient characteristic of community-university partners who have matured in their relationship is a shared authority in knowledge generation. Greenwood (2008) describes this occasion as collaborative arenas for knowledge development in which the professional researcher's knowledge is combined with the local knowledge of the stakeholders in defining the problem to be addressed. Together, they design and implement the actions to be taken on the basis of their shared understanding of the problem. Together, the parties develop plans of action to improve the situation together, and they evaluate the adequacy of what was done. (p. 327).

We began to experience this share knowledge generation in our partnership when writing a culturally responsive program evaluation. Data collection methods were crafted to fit Padres' culture and ways of knowing. Interviews were replaced with cultural circles and dialogue. Art, metaphors, and storytelling became vehicles of expression. Data pools became collections of life stories, reflections on practice, tales of self growth, and expressions of social challenges and commitments. The final product reflected the kind of knowledge that could only be possible when we brought our multiple epistemologies together.

We hope that the writing of this co-authored book mirrors our commitment to equity in epistemology. Respecting people's way of knowing is both a moral enterprise and an educational ideal (Sullivan, 2000). Thus, keeping foremost in our minds the diverse audiences engaging with this text (community members, university students and faculty), we crafted an architectural design of each chapter to include multiple ways of knowing. Each chapter begins with stories from the community and follows up with an academic discussion. By punctuating the readings with questions and activities, we invite you to engage in dialogue, reflection, and practice. We hope that doing this facilitates the coexistence of many peoples' epistemologies in the reading of this text, including Chapman's partners, Padres' partners, and yours. By embracing this multilogical and equitable venture in your own particular context, you may discover new ways of knowing, cohabiting, and being in this world. We assert that when enacting an ethic of epistemological equity, being *together* means knowing newly and knowing *together* means becoming new.

LET'S CHAT
CAFECITO II (Individual or Dialogue)

Have you ever read a book and then talked it over with a friend?

Did you learn something new about the book that you have not known before?

Activity

Share your favorite memory with a friend of something you learned in school. Examine the conditions and context of that memory to determine what made it a good learning experience. Analyze that learning experience by answering these questions:

What knowledge is important?
Whose knowledge is important?
Who does this knowledge benefit?

What did you learn from your friends and their perspectives of good learning? How has this new knowledge enriched your knowledge?

References

Berryman, M., SooHoo, S., & Nevin, A. (2013). *Culturally responsive methodologies:* Emerald Group Publishing Limited.

Cormier, D. (2011). Rhizomatic learning – why we teach? *Dave's Educational Blog: Building a better rhizome.* Retrieved from Dave's Educational Blog: Building a better rhizome website: http://davecormier.com/edblog/2011/11/05/rhizomatic-learning-why-learn/

Hall, B. L. (2015). *Beyond epistemicide: Knowledge democracy and higher education.* Paper presented at the International Symposium on Higher Education in the Age of Neo Liberalism and Audit Cultures, University of Regina.

Kincheloe, J. (2008). *Critical pedagogy.* New York, NY: Peter Lang.

King, J. (2017). Morally engaged research/ers dismantling epistemological nihilation in the age of impunity. *Educational Researcher, 46*(5), 211-222. doi: 10.3102/0013189X17719291

Shor, I., & Freire, P. (1987). *A pedagogy for liberation: Dialogues on transforming education* (Kindle ed.): Bergin & Garvey Publishers.

Sullivan, W.M. 2000. "Institutional identity and social responsibility in Higher Education." In T. Ehrlich (Ed.), *Civic Responsibility and Higher Education*, Phoenix: Oryx Press, 19-36.

White, R. E., Cooper, K., & Mackey, W. (2014). Culturally relevant education and critical pedagogy: Devolution of hierarchies of power.Revista Internacional de Educación para la Justicia Social, 3(2), 123-140.

Section 2: Becoming

At the midpoint of our coming to know each other, Padres Unidos and Chapman began to understand ourselves in a context of becoming and an *ontology of possibility*. Our collective confidence in the credo of *anything is possible* is rooted in a core belief that people, through collective effort, can change the way we understand the world and manifest this understanding into actual change. Paulo Freire (1998) refers to this concept as *becoming*, where, through "conscious human action in the world" (Anderson, 2016, para. 3), humanity strives toward completion through ethical relationships with each other. As a consequence, within the foundational status of relationships, becoming implies a dynamic understanding of the world and its continual change as collaborators negotiate the terms of their lived experiences. The dynamism suggests that the nature of human life is toward change rather than staying the same, which bears the potential of transformation, or *hope*. Nita Freire (2014) clarifies the transformative potential of becoming when she discusses its counterpart, untested feasibility:

> *"The concept of untested-feasibility provides the necessary unity of this lucid, joy, and transparency of the dream, in which ontologically human process is presented as possible."*

Freire's (2014) expression articulates the relationship between hope and potential, as the dream of a better future can be actualized through collective effort, which is fundamental to the human experience. The concept of *becoming* is related to several integral pieces of the Padres Unidos and Chapman University partnership, including the centrality of sharing power through non-hierarchal organizational structures. Hierarchy popularly refs to the power structure of public or private institutions (Bookchin, 2005). These organizations commonly have a CEO or president at the top of structure and a multitude of tiered positions below. The differentiated power among individuals may potentially upset the possibility of equitable relationships. Further, Bookchin (2005) warns that the consideration of hierarchy should not be limited to state or private institutions, as "hierarchy and domination could easily continue to exist in a 'classless' or 'stateless' society… [with] domination of the young by the old, of women by men, of one ethnic group by another, …of countryside by town" (p. 68). Bookchin (2005) advocates for a framework of *social ecology*, which emphasizes the interconnectedness and interdependence of people with each other, as well as with nature. Within this frame, hierarchies are difficult to maintain as every being is equally important to the constitution of the whole. Bookchin (2005) conceptualizes social ecology in terms consistent with Freire's notion of *becoming*, "social ecology… is a concept of an ever-developing universe, indeed a vast process of achieving wholeness" (p. 11).

Padres Unidos realized the potential of *becoming* through their teaching practices of "circles of love." Conceived as something reminiscent of Freire's (2004) cultural circles, circles of love are dialogue-driven teaching, learning, and conversational groups. Cultural circles were developed as a space where participants could begin to unravel their social context and connect in the language of the people with political and existential worries (Gadotti, 1994, p. xiii). Importantly, the circles of love emphasize shared power, joint decision making, collaboration, and are foundational to facilitating an organization that prioritizes relationships.

Beyond their own organization, the emphasis on the maintenance of relationships was integral to Padres Unidos' relationship with community members and Chapman University. Captured by the phrase *walking with them*, members often articulate their desire to enter into deeply empathetic relationships with others by ever-striving toward understanding the people or organizations that they work with. Realized in their teaching practices, curriculum is tailored to the interests, perspectives, and cultural context of those with whom they work. In the field of education, the concept is related to Freire's development of generative themes, where the curriculum is co-developed with the participant in local contexts (Gadotti, 1994). Considered broadly within the context of the social ecology frame, *walking with them* helps promote a sense of resiliency as members learn to collaborate with each other and the community learns to enact change.

Within the *ontology of possibility*, the Padres Unidos and Chapman University partnership fosters the sense of hope. As an organization, Padres Unidos helps their membership and community partners understand their role in creating and promoting change. The Chapman University partners, with a common sense of the centrality of relationships in building a better future, have endeavored to challenge hierarchal obstacles commonly placed between the university and community. The obstacles are related to a hierarchy of epistemology, or the way of coming to know the world, where university members' knowledge is popularly more valued than the community's. Where these hierarchies are successfully and continually challenged, universities and communities can *become* together, imbuing hope for a better tomorrow.

The following section will describe the forgoing concepts in more detail. Each passage is related to the broader theme of *becoming* and is rooted in the words and stories of members of Padres Unidos. The first chapter describes **Walking with Them** and the role that the concept plays in framing Padres Unidos and their collaboration with partners. The second chapter describes **Communal Structures** and the centrality of power-sharing between organizations. The following chapter describes the partnership's use of **Dialogue and Cultural Circles** and how they have affected the structure of our mutual work. The fourth chapter describes how the relationships fostered in the dialogue circles and between the organizations created spaces of **Teaching and Learning**. The fifth chapter describes how **Resiliency and Resourcefulness** are the grit that it takes to sustain one's self amidst poverty and social challenges.

References

Anderson, J. (2016). Paulo Freire's philosophy of education and our ontological incompleteness. *The Partially Examined Life*. Retrieved from The Partially Examined Life: A philosophy podcast and philosophy blog website: https://partiallyexaminedlife.com/2016/08/30/paulo-freires-philosophy-of-education-and-our-ontological-incompleteness/

Bookchin, M. (2005). *The ecology of freedom: The emergence and dissolution of hierarchy.* Oakland, CA: AK Press.

Freire, N. (2014). *The presence of Paulo Freire at Chapman University.* Paper presented at the Re-Dedication of the Paulo Freire Critical Pedagogy Archives, Chapman University, Orange California.

Freire, P. (1998). *Pedagogy of freedom: Ethics, democracy, and civic courage:* Rowman & Littlefield Publishers.

Freire, P. (2004). *Pedagogy of the oppressed.* New York, NY: Continuum.

Gadotti, M. (1994). *Reading Paulo Freire: His life and work.* New York, New York: State University of New York Press.

WALKING WITH

Story: Duck Formation

The familiar V flight formation of ducks and other migratory birds has fascinated people over time. The precision and grace of this aerial choreography have inspired many folks to consider its metaphoric meanings of collaboration, community, leadership, teamwork and alliance. It is Mother Nature's signature of unity and *us-ness* monographed in the sky. The V flight formation broadcasts for all to witness, the power and the majesty of *togetherness*.

Padres Unidos has observed from its perch that, when a bird is tired or injured, some birds join it while others move up to take its place. The injured bird is never alone or abandoned. The support birds stay with it until it recovers and is ready to resume its position.

Sometimes the lead bird falls back. According to Patricia Huerta, Padres Unidos' head organizer, it takes true humility for a leader to recognize the strength of her fellow members so that she can stand back for others to lead while repositioning one's self in an organization.

LET'S CHAT
CAFECITO I (Individual or Dialogue)

As a leader, how do you recognize the leadership skills of others?

How do you know:
when to stand alone?
when you need others to support you?
when you need to support others?

Discussion

Walking with is the way that Padres Unidos describes the methodology of its cultural workers in their community. *Walking with* means working with fellow parents through whatever problems or concerns they bring to the organization. From the beginning of a program, recruitment for new classes means *walking* door-to-door and letting people know about class offerings. The *walking with* approach can literally mean walking with parents to medical appointments or shelters. It also means developing organic curricula based on the unique complexities of assets and benefits within diverse community groups.

Walking with is more than operations, it is also a day-to-day ethical goal. In the prefigurative tradition, a movement to cultivate strong democracies, consciously informing daily activities with a clearly defined ethical goal is seen as an essential aspect of social transformation (Breines, 1989). Within the prefigurative tradition, social change occurs *within* relationships between people or institutions. This perspective is rooted in the understanding that people create the world through collaboration from the bottom up, with the goal of flattening hierarchies. Therefore, to *walk with* means to walk as equals. By doing so, we create a better world through the equitable nature of the *process itself* (Graeber, 2007, 2013).

Inspired by spiritual and cultural traditions of service, Padres Unidos embraces an engaged community approach. It is the same ethical process (a prefigurative process) that is found in a story well known to many in the community, the Exodus. It is the story of a people who become who they are as they walk together in the desert with each other and with the divine. The people of the Exodus pass through the sea from Egypt into the desert to start a new journey toward freedom. The group had no single unifying identity other than that of

48

historical oppression. Desperately dependent on one another, they wander in the desert without knowing what lies ahead. The walking is more than simply steps along a path, it is a process of self-discovery as the people begin to form a new communal identity as sojourners.

The patterns of becoming and transforming, welcoming and refining, learning and sojourning, which are evident in the biblical narrative, are also found in Padres Unidos. It is a modern-day community which is *walking with* those who have found themselves in the deserts of life. Despite connections which may have existed before Padres began, none of its members have ever known each other in the way that they are coming to know each other through the work of this community. With every new step, the members of Padres are discovering who they are as a community of equals and companions on the road of life.

The egalitarian commitment of Padres Unidos found resonance with the ethical philosophy of university partners. Dr. Suzanne SooHoo's reflective notes show this kinship:

> *Before I can walk, I must stand. As an academic and activist, I am not a neutral dispassionate researcher. I am deeply committed to effecting change with our local community members in ethical and culturally responsive ways. With research steeped in colonizing tradition, I deliberately contemplate how I **stand up** for humanizing methodologies, **stand for** equity and social justice, **stand with** the people and **stand by** as partner and ally. I learn to stand when faced with limit situations that challenge my ability to understand what it is that I understand. Only then am I worthy to walk with others.*

This commitment to justice, informed by humility and critical analysis, meant that university partners valued work that was culturally responsive and politically responsible. Although *walking with them* was not the terminology of these researchers, it was a foundational ethic.

This ethic informed the creation of this book. It is the result of Padres parents and Chapman researchers walking together. Research started with shared conversations in the opening of a rich relationship. The partnership solidified itself in visits to schools, juvenile halls, organizers' homes, community centers, university/professional conferences, committees and classes — walking, studying and co-participating in each other's spaces — learning each other's world view.

Taking *walking with them* seriously, we have moved from a position of respectful co-existence in our work to the co-creation of new knowledge in the writing of this book. In intentional mutuality, we have been sharing and reflecting on the values and knowledge which are unique to this partnership. It is a shared knowing and being, a new phase of our relationship as equal partners. Like the V formation of migratory birds and the methodology of Padres itself, we have been transformed by a prefigurative commitment to walking and working as a more equitable version of us.

LET'S CHAT
CAFECITO II (Individual or Dialogue)

In the community, there may be times where you will need to differentiate among leading, following and power sharing/walking with them.

What benefits/drawbacks does an egalitarian leveling of power have in building new relationships?

How would you operationalize this approach?

How might the concept of walking with them inform your future work in communities?

Activity

Learning Walk (inspired by Horton and Freire (1990) *We Make the Road by Walking*)
"Walking is a pedagogy for learning" (Guajardo, Guajardo, Janson, & Militello, 2016, p. 98). The word pedagogy has Greek origins that means to lead a child.

Debrief a learning episode by walking and talking instead of just talking. Did the walk enhance the nature of the discussion? Why or why not?

References

Breines, W. (1989). *Community and organization in the new left, 1962-1968*. New Brunswick, UK: Rutgers University Press.

Graeber, D. (2007). *Possibilities: Essays on hierarchy, rebellion, and desire*. Oakland, CA: AK Press.

Graeber, D. (2013). *The democracy project: A history, a crisis, a movement*: Penguin Books, Limited.

Guajardo, M. A., Guajardo, F., Janson, C., & Militello, M. (2016). *Reframing community partnerships in education: Uniting the power of place and wisdom of people*. New York, NY: Routledge.

Horton, M., & Freire, P. (1990). *We make the road by walking: Conversations on education and social change* Philadelphia, PA: Temple University Press.

COMMUNAL STRUCTURES

Story: Juncos Plants

They are reed-like plants called juncos and when you are going through the hills in some part of Mexico, you will see them. They're pretty tall, taller than me and thin and there are many of them. We saw them on the way to town. The fields were filled with what looked like sugar canes. When we were coming back, the plants were gone. I asked a person who lived in the hills, "How can that be?" The guy said, "They are gone because it's windy right now. The plants all bend down because it's windy and they return standing when the wind is gone." I saw this with my own eyes.

LET'S CHAT
CAFECITO I (Individual or Dialogue)

What are some examples where flexibility is important in your life? In your family? At work? In your social life?

Why is it important to remain flexible?

Discussion

There are many ways to understand organizations. Many of us are accustomed to hierarchical structures of organization. Acceptance or simple awareness of other ways of organizing expands the degrees of freedom one can experience in an interconnected world (Wilson, 1998).

Looking at our world through the lens of a living system, we can see how the juncos story illustrates the advantage of flexibility for surviving an external climate. A similar moral applies to the survival of organizations that can "flex" to adjust to changing social or political climates that may otherwise harm an organization. In the business world, organizations that are able to adjust to market forces in an ever-changing economy are the ones that survive and thrive. A holacratic business model (Robertson, 2015) is sympathetic to the juncos metaphor in that the flat-organizational structure is more adaptable to market forces than traditional top-down structures that tend to be more rigid. In a holacracy, the employees are given the flexibility to make decisions independently. The day-to-day practices of the employee are informed by the long-term and midterm goals of the organization and the employees are not beholden to layers of bureaucratic management. Therefore, the primary mode of "governance" in a holacracy comes from meetings or dialogues in which members collectively make decisions, share resources, and ensure that the organization is effectively moving forward. However, while holacracy presents a departure from "business as usual" in the world of commerce, it may not do enough to challenge the innate power disparity between communities and universities.

As a response, Padres Unidos and university researchers chose collaborative and communal structures to strive toward equity. From a social political lens, groups that are organized to serve those who are marginalized or disenfranchised in society may decide to avoid replicating dominant "power over" structures. Instead, more democratic structures can achieve the goal of optimizing unrealized potential and discovering personal and collective agency. Both Padres Unidos and the university researchers operate on the premise that our work is *with* people, helping people help themselves. As social scientists, we see our research as a means to serve the community, working with them to address problems they have identified as important to them.

Padres Unidos and Chapman researchers adapted its organizational structures and curriculum to reflect the lived experiences and rich cultural capital of our participants. A flat organizational structure enabled us to share meals, share values, and share governance within a context of reciprocal humanity.

The value of reciprocation and power sharing is based on a principle known as mutualism. The concept applies to the reimagining of structures based on ensuring that the *process* of an organization mirrors the ethical goals. In the context of outlining social values, Suissa (2010) describes mutualism as an "insight that society should be organized not on the basis of a hierarchical, centralist, top-down structure such as the state, but on the basis of reciprocal voluntary agreements between individuals" (p. 11). The nature of the reciprocal relationship can be found in the participants' (both university and community members) willingness to modify their beliefs, circumstances, and/or practices and the relationship developed. Significantly, the relational aspect of mutualism avoids hyper-individualism by ensuring that the collective is as important as the individual.

The partnership strengthens both entities as it exchanges resources and feedback. Academic and community wisdom share a symbiotic relationship. Similar to living biological systems, social ecology evolves when an inadequacy is apparent. When systems become aware that they need something more than they have now, they seek new means to survive. Our sustainability can be measured by our flexibility and our ability to enrich the experiences of all of those within our organization while making it a more resilient to external forces.

A Note About the Title of this Chapter

Language shapes thought (Vygotsky & Kozulin, 1986). Therefore, the choice of words to represent our preferred and desired form of organizing meant identifying words that represent a truthfulness of our human-centered governance structure. It is extremely difficulty to craft new language to symbolize our transformed realities as a result of this partnership.

This chapter has had many names, and status quo thinking prevented us from accurately describing our democratic, culturally responsive, and nonhierarchical ways of working. The issue demonstrates that the dominance of English language colonization is so powerful that one often cannot think beyond vertical organization charts or the antonym of hierarchy when describing governance systems. Indigenous scholar Four Arrows reminds us, "How we discuss the world creates social realities" (Four Arrows, 2016, p. 98), so in the spirit of aligning our actions with our beliefs, we chose *Communal Structures,* borrowed from our examination of biosystems, because those words described the working relationships of our partnership more truthfully.

LET'S CHAT
CAFECITO II (Individual or Dialogue)

In your community organization:
Who makes the decisions? How are decisions made? With whom?

Who are the powerbrokers? Women? Men? Elders? Youth? Does the official organization chart reflect the day-to-day operations? What adaptations are made and why?

Activity
As you approach the community, flexibility and open mindedness are necessary dispositions to new experiences and ways of viewing the world. We must be equally comfortable with both hierarchical and other schemas of organization. Conduct a mini-ethnographic study and review the way your organization operates. Does the organizational structure reflect the values of the organization? What suggestions would you make to align values with governance structure?

References

Four Arrows. (2016). *Point of departure: Returning to our more authentic worldview for education and survival.* Charlotte, NC: Information Age Publishing.

Robertson, B. J. (2015). *Holacracy: The new management system for a rapidly changing world.* New York, NY: Henry Holt and Co..

Suissa, J. (2010). *Anarchism and education: A philosophical perspective.* Oakland, CA: PM Press.

Vygotsky, L., & Kozulin, A. (1986). *Thought and language.* Boston, MA: MIT.

Wilson, E. O. (1998). *Consilience: The unity of knowledge.* New York, NY: Vintage Books.

DIALOGUE & CULTURAL CIRCLES

Story: What Do You See?

The multipurpose room buzzed with chatter as the women gathered for class and sat around nine large round tables. Their young preschool children were coloring and playing with educational blocks and toys on the far side of the room. Padres Unidos' preschool instructors chaperoned the little ones. A facilitator at each table placed hand mirrors at each of the six seats in preparation for the session. When class began, the facilitator asked the women, "When you look in the mirror, what do you see?" The room grew quiet as the women thoughtfully examined their faces. They scrutinized the shape of their features, the color of their hair, the texture of their skin and commented on what they considered imperfections: acne, creases, coloration.

"Who is that person?" the facilitator asked.

A woman shared, "I see a broken person." Tears slowly rolled down her face. Another woman sobbed, "I see a person who has failed her family." One more woman revealed, "I don't know what to do anymore." One can hear the gentle opening of hearts across the tables as the curriculum for the day's class emerges.

LET'S CHAT
CAFECITO I (Individual or Dialogue)

Imagine you are sitting at the table. What do you think would be the ensuing conversation at that table?

What dialogue can happen in circle formation that cannot happen in other configurations?

What experiences have you had in dialogue circles?

How are you a mirror for others in your circle?

What are the ways that others serve as a mirror to you?

Discussion

Watching the Padres Unidos class described in our story unfold, Chapman University researchers likened the lesson to the use of Freirean cultural circles. Critical educators Lake and Kress (2017) refer to cultural circles as learning environments in which the people themselves contribute their lived experiences to the content of the curriculum by raising issues of importance in their lives. Cultural circles do *not* include lectures or syllabi. Rather, content emerges from the lived experiences of participants. People bring their funds of knowledge to these spaces and together reveal, unpack, and make-sense through shared experience. It is a space of dialogue.

Dialogue is different that chatting. Chatting is an informal exchange. "Dialogue represents a powerful and transformative political process of interaction between people. It requires the interactive and ongoing participation *with* and *among* people" (Darder, 2002, p. 103). "In genuine dialogue we come to understand others' perspectives and do not seek to indoctrinate others with our own perceptions and biases. Dialogue is the encounter between people, mediated by the world in which they live… in order to name the world" (Allen,

2007, p. 68). Indeed, "Dialogue requires an intense faith in (others), faith in their power to make and remake, to create and re-create, faith in (their) vocation to be more fully human (which is not the privilege of an elite but the birthright of all)" (Freire, 1970, p. 46). Clearly, dialogue is much richer than mere conversation and it finds a home in cultural circles (Allen, 2007).

"Cultural circles" is not the term used by all who practice dialogue-in-the-round. Similar configurations are referred to as *healing circles* or *community circles*. Padres Unidos uses the term *Love Circles* in their education programs to describe these instructional formations. No matter the name, these circles are spaces of meaning-making for all involved. Participants in these dialogical spaces are seen and interact as equals. The ideological and physical formation of these circles help groups to maintain equitable participation and to value individual voice. Physically, they are arranged to permit equal access to dialogue from any seat. This affords all individuals an opportunity to listen and speak.

Like Padres Unidos' classes, doctoral seminars at Chapman also favor dialogue circles because of the equity involved. Both Chapman and Padres Unidos typically think of teachers as facilitators or conveners rather than leaders. "In cultural circles, participants' experiences are invited, valued, and central to the construction of meaning" (Souto-Manning, 2010, p. 19). Regular rearrangement of classroom furniture into circles communicates responsibility as well as equity. Here, responsibility means bringing your histories, cultures, and languages (often estranged) with you. Within these circular formations, participants create social and political space for new ways of knowing and becoming while abandoning traditional performances in lecture-style classrooms.

Cultural circles can be transformative. Their use by educators echo Emmy Award winning filmmaker

Lois Farfel Stark's (forthcoming) assertion that, "living in new shapes reshapes our thinking." Mind, body and spirit are liberated to move and act, learn and question differently. One can feel that the energy in the room is different from what many people say replaces the voice of one. Studies (Alexander, 2017; Mercer, 2008) have shown that the more students talk, the more they learn. When teachers or leaders dominate conversations, they diminish optimizing student/participant engagement. Cultural circles promote democratic and compassionate participation in the rich practice of dialogue.

Through our own use of these circles, we as co-researchers have been transformed. Honoring dialogue was central to the success and sustainability of the Chapman University–Padres Unidos Partnership. Through dialogical relationships, university and community partners learn "to build learning communities through cultural circles in which they freely give voice to our thoughts, ideas, and perceptions about what we know and what we are attempting to understand" (Darder, 2002, p. 103). Dialogue enabled us to build and maintain relationships as we came to know each other as partners. Ours is a relationship that was forged while sitting together in many circles where dialogue has thrived. Thus, we end this chapter with a tribute to the circle itself:

> "Everything an Indian does is in a circle, and that is because the power of the World always works in circles, and everything tries to be round... The sky is round and I have heard the earth is round like a ball, and so are all the stars. The wind in its greatest power whirls, birds make their nest in circles, for theirs is the same religion as ours. The sun comes forth and goes down again in a circle. The moon does the same and both are round. Even the seasons form a great circle in their changing, and always come back again to where they were. Our teepees were round like the nests of birds. And they were always set in a circle, the nation's hoop." — Chief Black Elk (2018)

LET'S CHAT
CAFECITO II (Individual or Dialogue)

Where in your work, school or community settings might you recommend dialogue or cultural circles?

What conditions or purposes might these formations serve?

Make a list of when it is useful to convene in hierarchical formations and when it is to convene in dialogical/ cultural circles.

Activity

Present two mini presentations on the same topic: one that is designed as a lecture and one that is designed for people to engage in dialogue cultural circles. Compare the two presentations. What advantages or disadvantages did each configuration have?

References

Alexander, R. (2017). Dialogic teaching and the study of classroom talk: A developmental bibliography. Robin Alexander.org. Retrieved from Dialogic Teaching website: http://www.robinalexander.org.uk/dialogic-teaching/

Allen, J. (2007). *Creating welcoming schools: A practical guide to home school partnerships with diverse families.* New York, NY: Teachers College Press.

Chief Black Elk. (2018). Chief Black Elk: Quotes by Chief Black Elk. Retrieved Dec. 6, 2017 from https://www.goodreads.com/author/show/16968754.Chief_Black_Elk

Darder, A. (2002). *Reinventing Paulo Freire: A pedagogy of love.* Boulder, CO: Westview Press.

Freire 1970 - Freire, P. (1970). *Pedagogy of the oppressed.* New York, NY: Continuum.

Lake, R., & Kress, T. (2017). Mamma don't put that blue guitar in a museum: Greene and freire's duet of radical hope in hopeless times. *Review of Education, Pedagogy, and Cultural Studies, 39*(1), 60-75.

Mercer, N. (2008). The seeds of time: Why classroom dialogue needs a temporal analysis. *Journal of the Learning Sciences, 17*(1), 33-59.

Souto-Manning, M. (2010). The critical cycle. In M. Souto-Manning (Ed.), *Freire, teaching, and learning: Culture circles across contexts* (Vol. 350, pp. 29-45). New York, NY: Peter Lang AG.

Stark, L. F. (forthcoming). *The telling image: Shapes of changing times.* Austin, TX: Greenleaf Book Group Press.

TEACHING ♭ LEARNING

Copyright ©2018 SooHoo

Story: Jazz Man in the Music Class

It is another first day of school. And that marks the end of summer, the end of adventure, and the beginning of doldrums. Greg struggled through the morning talks about rules and homework that the teacher was giving. Boring!

When the bell rang for music class to start, he grabbed his recorder and walked down the hall to the classroom. The teacher wasn't there yet, but the students were already in their seats and waiting to play music.

A new teacher walked in and stood in front of the class and asked what they learned the previous year. Greg raised his hand, stood up, and played "Hot Cross Buns." All the other students joined him. Note for note, they played the music just as had been taught.

The teacher asked them to keep playing as she also raised a recorder to her lips. Suddenly she started to riff on the sounds of the monotone music. She asked them to do the same. The teacher later explained, "This is jazz. In jazz, we play and make new music *together*." Greg's eyes grew big as he listened to the new sounds they were making. School would never be the same!

LET'S CHAT
CAFECITO I (Individual or Dialogue)

In a conventional classroom structure, who decides what you will learn?

If you could restructure the classroom like a jazz band, who would decide what learning is important?

In jazz, we can bring our whole hearts to the music experience. Can you name educational experiences where you had a similar opportunity?

Discussion

Traditionally, universities are simply refined examples of secondary and elementary classrooms. Professors are the experts imparting the most essential elements of knowledge into the minds of the learners (Freire, 1970). Part of successful admission into the university requires that one has *learned to learn* in such a system of teaching.

Progressive and critical educators at the university have long resisted the dominance of transmission models of teaching and learning where the teacher is considered the dispenser of knowledge and students are passive, compliant learners. This approach to teaching can silence the contributions and interests that students bring with them to the classrooms. For years, Chapman University instructors have researched and studied alternative paradigms, dialogical strategies, and student-centered pedagogy, where students and teachers were equally engaged as both teachers and learners together.

We considered ourselves to have a reasonable amount of scholarly expertise. Imagine our surprise (revealing our entitled privilege), when we were invited to observe Padres Unidos' teaching practices and found their practices *matched* ours. How had they developed or acquired these teaching methods and why had we considered them epistemological foreigners? This phenomenon drew us to better understand what fundamental beliefs led to the striking similarities in teaching pedagogy. What follows is what we found as we looked deeply and across time.

Padre's methodology in teaching was one of commitment to an organic curriculum. Learners regularly shaped and directed the content of curriculum by raising issues of importance in their lives. Their objective to achieve personal and social consciousness was facilitated by love circles, a version of culture circles (Lake & Kress, 2017), which are primarily dialogical in nature as community workers and students alike problem pose and problem solve.

Problem-posing/problem-solving sessions are peppered with questions like these: "What happened?" "What is the source of the problem?" "What conditions cause this to happen? "What were the consequences?" "Can we see other possible ways to address this situation?" "What could we try to do?" "How can we communicate better to our loved ones?" Padres' repertoire of teaching methods included but were not limited to love circles, role-play, films, hugging, food, mindfulness breathing exercises, metaphors, and storytelling.

Consistent with the prioritization of participant voice, Padres' curriculum is derived from the community members themselves. Like Freire's (1970) generative themes, where instruction is rooted in local knowledge and practices, Padres Unidos develops their organic curriculum from the needs and interests of those whom they serve. Within Padres Unidos, all of the teacher-facilitators were once students in Padres themselves. This means that they brought their own subjectivities and storied lives as courageous survivors of poverty, immigration, and abuse into their instructional repertoires.

With compassion and unwavering patience, they committed to assist and support their fellow community members in hardship. Beyond the classroom, Padres educators were the "go-to" people who provided information and personal support to families in the community who needed to know where to go for health and school issues. They serviced more than 25 elementary schools in the Santa Ana Unified School District and Mission Viejo Unified School District, at Boys and Girls Clubs, the Catholic Archdiocese and at Orange County Juvenile

Hall. They served as educators, healers, caretakers, storytellers, communication advisors, and social workers. Their goal was to build strong families who could build strong communities.

One cannot understand the nature of this partnership without understanding Padres' and Chapman's shared pedagogical ethic. Chapman researchers present frames of democratic education and critical pedagogy. They also bring experiences from their doctoral seminars, where students routinely are invited and expected to actively engage in theory and practice of not only topics of human and social phenomena but also of their own learning environments and study conditions at the university. These students are regularly involved in problem posing, voicing their perspectives, and participating in dialogical cultural circles that recognize the possibilities and limitations of unexplored potential, referred to as "untested feasibility" (Freire, 1970). It is in these contexts that we can acknowledge our own "unfinishedness" (Freire, 1970) about each other's worlds and our collective process of "becoming" together.

Like a fractal or the net of Indra, where each crystal is reflected in all of the others, the philosophy of teaching within both organizations is a mirror reflection of the larger partnership. Principles of relational and critical consciousness are central to both groups, both individually and collectively, within the larger partnership. Whether one is in a classroom or at the partnership table, there is an invitation for people's lived realities to be a part of the curriculum. There is a dialogical experience, an acknowledgement of human agency and unrecognized potential, and a community of support available to individuals within a context of trust and compassion. While these instructional beliefs replicate themselves with faithful consistency, each lesson is different and uniquely tethered to the collective experiences, synergies, and capacities of those who are present.

Teaching is something that happens between community members, as is the act of learning. To be with another in authenticity is to enter into a pedagogical space. As such, we have come to see how our own partnership has been (and will continue to be) an extended moment of teaching and learning together. The partnership has transformed us from two distinct groups into a single teaching-learning community, discovering together and being led by the experience of being one, making music together.

LET'S CHAT
CAFECITO II (Individual or Dialogue)

What would a classroom space look like if teaching was like a jazz band?

How would you develop a curriculum that incorporates the talent and experiences that students bring to the classroom?

Activity

Use the Padres Unidos problem-posing/problem-solving questions in one of your small group conversations. How effective are these questions in opening the dialogue and addressing community, social or academic issues? What would you change or modify to accommodate your specific context?

References

Freire, P. (1970). *Pedagogy of the oppressed.* NY: Continuum.

Kirylo, J.D. & Boyd, D. (2017). *Paulo Freire: His faith, spirituality, and theology.* The Netherlands: Sense Publishers.

Lake, R. & Kress, T. (2017). Mamma don't put that blue guitar in a museum: Greene and Freire's duet of radical hope in hopeless times. *Review of Education, Pedagogy, and Cultural Studies.* 39:1. 60-75

RESILIENCY & RESOURCEFULNESS

Story: The Donkey

One day a farmer's donkey fell into an abandoned well. The animal cried piteously for hours as the farmer tried to figure out what to do. Finally, he decided the animal was old and the well needed to be covered up anyway; so it just wasn't worth it to try to retrieve the donkey.

He invited all his neighbors to come over and help him. They each grabbed a shovel and began to shovel dirt into the well. Realizing what was happening, the donkey at first cried and wailed horribly. Then, a few shovelfuls later, he quieted down completely.

The farmer peered down into the well and was astounded by what he saw. With every shovelful of dirt that hit his back, the donkey was doing something amazing. He would shake it off and take a step up on the new layer of dirt. As the farmer's neighbors continued to shovel dirt on top of the animal, he would shake it off and take a step up. Pretty soon, the donkey stepped up over the edge of the well and trotted off, to the shock and astonishment of all the neighbors.

Life is going to shovel dirt on you, all kinds of dirt. The trick to getting out of the well is to not let it bury you, but to shake it off and take a step up. Each of our troubles is a stepping stone.

LET'S CHAT
CAFECITO I (Individual or Dialogue)

Have you experienced a time where you felt over-burdened by life's challenges?

What did you learn about yourself? Share your story with a friend.

What did you do to address those challenges?

Did you learn something from sharing your story?

Discussion

Padres Unidos originated from the journey of one immigrant family that drew strength from overcoming hardship (Huerta, 2014). Patricia Huerta is a mother of six and founder of Padres Unidos. Her personal journey reflects the experiences of many of the community members of Santa Ana, California. Huerta (2014) tells the story of how she came to the United States under duress in 1976. The transition to living in Santa Ana, California was difficult, as Huerta (2014) explained. "Making the switch between the homeland and a foreign country is very difficult for migrants" (p. 118). Aspects of the difficulty come from unfamiliarity with the system, making enough money to survive, finding jobs, and securing food and shelter (Huerta, 2014). However, she also explained that her history of overcoming struggles as an immigrant helped build relationships that brought hope to the Santa Ana community.

Huerta (2014) described two related paths on her journey, one educational and the other spiritual, that intersected to develop the Padres Unidos program. The ethic that bound her to her journey was service to others. While the process was difficult, she could rely on the community and her faith that helped her "to grow and be the person who I could be" (Huerta, 2014, p. 118). Huerta went back to school to help her family. It was a struggle because she did not speak English and formerly had only received education up to middle school. Nonetheless, she started down the path of education by enrolling in a community college. Huerta described how her children and counselor helped her throughout the process, wherein her counselor encouraged her to keep moving forward, and her children had faith in her abilities to make it through the program. Their faith in Huerta's abilities proved to be well placed. Upon graduating from community college, she went on to pursue a master's degree in social work where she "graduated with honors, at the top" of her class (Huerta, 2014, p. 119).

While transitioning to life in the United States, Huerta (2014) explained that she found solace in the Catholic Church. Huerta found that the Church was a comforting place where she could grieve. In fact, she would visit a local parish frequently throughout the week. She explains that the priest helped her become more involved in the church and that her involvement blossomed into a deep commitment to the community. She would become a regular participant in the life of the Church and a catechist, or religious education teacher.

The classes Patricia Huerta taught in the church were very successful and popular with the community. The number of parent participants in her classes increased from 80 to more than 500 in just a three-month period. Her classes would become Padres Unidos, focusing on parenting by means of an education that reached the whole family. Huerta (2014) explained that she could successfully teach these programs with her family because of commonly shared experiences with the participants. "We understand where these people are coming from because we have been there too" (p. 119). Huerta maintains an ongoing relationship with the local Catholic diocesan programs which work with parents and families.

Patricia Huerta's story of resiliency alludes to an understanding of what it means to be *ethically* resilient. She demonstrates a profound sense of resiliency and resourcefulness, in the traditional sense of these terms, through her ability to turn potentially dire circumstances into prosperity. She uses her talents to help herself and her family to come back from the brink to thrive in American society. However, this interpretation of Huerta's resiliency does not do justice to the deeper ethical tradition from which it arises. Her ethic leads Huerta to understand that it is in her ability to help her family she is also able to help her community. She has been doing so for nearly two decades through Padres Unidos. This sense of resourcefulness can be linked to an understanding of society as an intricately, intimately, and inextricably connected system of interpersonal relationships.

The story of resiliency and resourcefulness has many chapters in the life of Padres Unidos. One of these is the collaboration that has been forged between the organization and Chapman University. Part of that relationship is the partnership that exist between researchers from the Paulo Freire Democratic Project and Padres Unidos. This partnership began with a mutual acceptance of an ethic that honored each other and the equitable relationship that could develop between us over time. Maintaining these ethical partnerships is partially dependent on the ability to adapt, accommodate, and empathize. This required self-reflection and a personal realignment of partners to adjust to one another in the negotiation of meanings and knowledge. The fruit of this work has been a transformative and vibrant partnership which is built upon relationships that benefit everyone. This partnership may not have necessitated resiliency and resourcefulness, but it became clear that the larger context in which the partnership existed, namely academic institutions and cultures, did require these attributes in order to negotiate. Collaborating with the larger university meant facing systemic challenges for Padres Unidos, just as coming into American society presented obstacles for its founder, Patricia Huerta.

Flowing from this research partnership, Padres Unidos and the university began to enter into new collaborations. Many of these have taken place through the mutual efforts of those in the research partnership, advocating and constructing possibilities for the community organization to be ever-closer connected to the university. Since that time, some of Padres' members are both students and faculty at the university with the development of a two-year Community Worker program located on the Chapman campus. Over 90 adult students have graduated from this program already. Padres' members are regularly invited guests and speakers at conferences, classes, workshops and symposia held by the College of Educational Studies and the Department of Sociology. Some members of the organization sit on a university committee tasked with the establishment of additional partnerships between local community organizations and the institution itself. Undergraduate and graduate assistant positions have been established and funded through university funding streams, which provide learners the opportunity to work with this local community organization. Yet, as wonderful as all this may seem, it has revealed a number of difficult realities. On whose terms are these taking place and with whose benefit in mind? Is relationship a central ethic across all these collaborations?

We believe that relationships are integral to maintaining an ethical partnership between communities and universities. The means of maintaining ethical partnerships is partially dependent on the institution's ability to adapt, accommodate, and empathize with community partners. When this adjustment does not take place, it results in inequitable conditions. For instance, Padres members who are faculty and students are primarily Latina women between the ages of 30 and 40, the same demographic represented by the custodial and food workers at the institution. As a result, like these workers, the adult students are treated as if they were functionally invisible. While they are visibly different, they are invisible as part of the student body, as for example, posters around campus showing student engagement do not include their images. They are treated with disbelief when they assert that they are students or adjunct faculty, having to show identification to have doors unlocked for regularly scheduled classes. Padres members regularly face micro-aggressions on campus events, as when people complain about the necessity of Spanish translation provisions for participants. Interactions outside of the research partnership with the university have, at times, led to frustration and hurt on the part of members of Padres.

Resiliency means to "continue forward in the face of adversity" (Zautra, Hall, Murray, & The Resilience Solutions Group, 2008, p. 132). Rather than giving up hope in the face of inequality, Padres has called upon its greatest resource, interpersonal relationships. The organization has maintained collaborations, strategically fostering relationships with key people at Chapman. On multiple occasions, the University president has joined Padres to celebrate their graduations, addressing the community in Spanish. He responded to the personal invitation of the organization to be partners in these spaces. Connections like these are ways of slowly building a shared understanding of collaboration for the road ahead. We believe that there are many routes to alignment of these two cultures and we are committed to making adjustments one episode, one person, and one relationship at a time.

Resourcefulness might be described as the flexible use of existing resources as well as creative ways of generating new resources for a given purpose. Padres shows this characteristic as it faces difficulties. Similar to all nonprofit organizations, Padres Unidos faces a regular sense of urgency of budget shortfalls, grant deadlines, and shortage of staffing. One year was particularly challenging. School board contracts were stalled due to delays in state budget allocations while, at the same time, private donations dried up. We were 3 weeks into the semester and our programs did not start. Out of this dire state emerged unexpected offers of support from the very students in the program themselves. Besides giving up all or some of their salaries, people offered, "I was going to get a new car but I can wait." "I was going to move into my own place instead of staying with my sister but it can wait." "We can make tamales and hot chocolate to sell at the school." People gathered at Patricia's house, assessed the organization's assets, and offered suggestions on how to raise money. University researchers volunteered to meet with schools and potential donors, to help with promotion and marketing strategies, and to assist with grant writing.

Resiliency and resourcefulness are important aspects of our partnership. Together we realize the inherent interdependence of the university and community in a truly equitable partnership. By acknowledging and utilizing our combined skills, experiences, and knowledge together, we develop deeper regard for resourcefulness and resiliency. Partnership and allyship begin to merge as our relationship is forged in the trials of difficulty while maintaining an unwavering hope. These occasions make us more resilient to external pressures that may seek to undermine the partnership. Together we protect the good work at hand in the midst of unforeseen odds.

LET'S CHAT
CAFECITO II (Individual or Dialogue)

What resources might you bring into a partnership (cultural, emotional, material, etc.)? How could you be open to recognizing underappreciated aspects of a partner as genuine resources?

What could organizations do to become more resilient and resourceful? What suggestions would you have to build into the culture of one of your organizations?

What cultural and ethical differences might need to be overcome for an institution to enter into an ethical relationship with a community-based movement?

Activity

Design a resiliency and resourcefulness plan by identifying the resources of your organization—social, economic, and political. After identifying your organization's resource capital (human and economic), compare it to the resources you employed for this year's organizational predictable and unforeseen challenges.

Which resources were valuable? Which resources were underutilized? What new resources were discovered? What possible collaborations or partnerships could strengthen your initiatives?

References

Huerta, P. (2014). Self-empowerment through grassroots efforts. In V. Carty, T. M. Woldemikael & R. Luevano (Eds.), *Scholars and southern californian immigrants in dialogue: New conversations in public sociology.* Plymouth, United Kingdom: Lexington Books.

Zautra, A. J., Hall, J. S., Murray, K. E., & The Resilience Solutions Group. (2008). Resilience: A new integrative approach to health and mental health research. *Health Psychology Review, 2*(1), 41-64.

SECTION 3
Belonging

Section 3: Belonging

The first two sections of this book sought to share what we have learned about the process of knowing and becoming. These chapters were crafted to move from encounter to learning, from experiencing the other to engaging with them. These are characteristic elements of the process of partnership between Padres Unidos and Chapman University. We have lived them from the time of our first introduction to this present moment. Experiencing this journey together has provided us with both problems and opportunities. These, in turn, have given birth to new questions about our relationship, knowledge, and purpose. One of the most important of these has been: What does it mean to belong to something?

On the surface, the question of belonging permits a relatively simple answer. Is not belonging simply affiliation with a group? But this also raises questions. How does one belong? Why does one belong? Are all forms of belonging the same? To what or whom do we belong by means of affiliation? The desire to belong is deep. bell hooks (1991) says that one of her greatest pains as a child was the sense that she did not belong. This desire to belong drives her work as a feminist theorist even today. She writes, "I came to theory desperate, wanting to comprehend — to grasp what was happening in the world and in me" (p. 1). Belonging begins with encountering the world and follows into learning about who we are in that world. It is an opaque concept, both tangible and illusive at once.

We believe, along with hooks, that the question of belonging is a philosophical one. Henry Taylor (1954) wrote that "Philosophy is not simply a subject to be studied. It is the process of sorting out principles and experiences and transforming them into new meanings" (p. 124). Only by pushing beyond the surface of our actions and knowledge can we come to truly understand the invisible thread that binds all these things together along with ourselves. Theorizing is not only something academics do, it is the birthright of all humans — the pondering and meaning making that contextualizes our lives (Craig, 2002). As Padres Chapman partners, we have often asked deep questions about what it means to belong to this partnership. These musings have helped us to understand ourselves as we come together. Whether our answers are couched in metaphor (our partnership is like a butterfly) or in academic language (our partnership is the enactment of an authentic democratic ethic), the result is always a more profound understanding.

We have shaded this section purple because all that is said here emerges from the mutual processes explained in the previous section of coming to know (teal) and becoming (red). The chapters are meant to elicit reflection of your own personal philosophies about relationships, research, and social action. We start with one of the deepest and most elusive realities that we have encountered in our work together: **spirituality.** Here we invite you to consider and be surprised by the ways that you and others may come to make sense of the world. Meaning-making constructs influence the way that people interact with each other and the world. In this partnership, we discovered that we shared a sense of **ethics and democracy** that guided our interactions with one another and society. The more that we continued to live and act according to these shared principles, the more we discovered that we grew in our belonging together. **Transformation and hope** were the characteristics which followed from our interactions. Every encounter mutually changed us and gave us new hope to persevere.

After exploring these key topics on the question of belonging, this section ends with a trilogy of chapters entitled: **scholarly activist, organic intellectual,** and **praxis of togetherness.** When reading these three chapters you will notice that the narrative which opens each story is the same. This is no mistake. Each section tells a story from a slightly different perspective. The lessons drawn from these stories bring light to what we have come to understand about our roles as academics and community members in relationship. In the first two of these chapters, we engage the possibility of restructuring the identities of "university researcher" and "community member" to align with an ethic of social justice. In the final chapter, we invite you to reconceptualize the role of relationships themselves in research. Imagine them, not as mechanisms to be utilized in creating ethical research, but as coterminous to the goal of the research itself. This centering of *relationship* radically moves it from the realm of mere method into a broader theoretical landscape. What if knowledge, validity, and action were simultaneous dependent on the authenticity of relationship? We propose that when the relationship becomes the true goal, then true belonging becomes possible and fruitful.

References

Craig, E. (2002). *Philosophy: A very short introduction.* New York, NY: Oxford University Press.

hooks, b. (1991). Theory as liberatory practice. *Yale Journal of Law & Feminism, 4*(1), 1-12.

Taylor, H. (1954). *On education and freedom.* New York, NY: Abelard-Schuman.

SPIRITUALITY

Story: Leaking Water Jug

Once upon a time, in ancient China, there was a young monk who drew water from the well and carried it back to the temple every day. The young monk carried two buckets of water slung on a bamboo pole across his shoulders.

One of the buckets was perfect while the other one was leaky, with several holes on the sides. Every time the young monk filled up the two buckets and got back to the temple, the leaky bucket would be half empty as water sprinkled out through the holes on its sides.

A villager asked the monk, "Why do you waste your time filling up the bucket with holes in it?" The young monk smiled slightly and nodded his head toward the road. "Look to the side of the road where the perfect bucket passed over. It is barren. Not even a blade of grass grows here." Pointing to blooming flowers on the other side of the road, the young monk said, "See these beautiful flowers? These are here because of the water that was sprinkled on the road each day. Had you not noticed them?"

LET'S CHAT
CAFECITO I (Individual or Dialogue)

Have you ever overlooked something important because you were focused elsewhere?

Has there ever been a time when you felt that someone failed to see a good work you did because they were looking for something else?

How did you feel on each of these occasions?

Discussion

When we focus on one thing, we often miss seeing the presence of something else. When the villager focused on the efficiency of the bucket, he failed to see the young monk's contribution to the flowers growing on the side of the road. Our focus can also be our blind spot.

Researchers wrestle with focus-blindness across all disciplines. For example, Toby Spribille (Gies, 2017), a lichenologist from the University of Alberta, shows how difficult this is when he talks about his breakthrough scientific discovery of finding a second fungus in many lichen. "When you're used to thinking there's just one fungus there, that's what you see… One of the most difficult things was allowing myself to have an open mind to the idea that 150 years of literature may have entirely missed the theoretical possibility that there would be more than one fungal partner in the lichen symbiosis" (pp. 57-58). Our frames of reference are limited to what we know. When we see something we don't understand, our curiosity and our openness to accept multiple perspectives allow us to see how different aspects of our world are related, networked, and integrated.

Admittedly, Chapman researchers began their work with Padres Unidos wearing a scientific lens. They were looking for the tangible, observable, transcribeable, and quantifiable evidence that would point to understanding Padres Unidos. In doing this, they sensed that there was something missing in their analysis, something that was present that they weren't catching. That "something" in this partnership was spirituality. The Chapman researchers didn't see "it" at first because they weren't looking for it. But it had been there all along. Once discovered, we recognized its grace and power to sustain Padres' work, particularly in limit situations (Freire, 2004).

Spirituality is not synonymous to religion, although it can be the enlivening soul of religious practice. For Padres Unidos, it is the animating, sustaining motivation and meaning of life which connects individuals and groups with something larger than themselves. Rather than an articulated ideology, it is the quiet backbone of this organization and can be found in situations that require renewed faith, hope, and resilience. In many ways, to concretize spirituality with a finite definition is to do violence to its ethereal essence. Yet, through faithful engagement in activities supporting their organization's mantra, "Successful Families Build Successful Communities," the members of Padres Unidos give evidence of their spiritual core.

In any given week, Padres members can be found teaching classes, delivering gift baskets, making community phone calls, acting as parent liaisons to the schools, escorting families to health and social agencies, and organizing community events. And while God was not mentioned explicitly, members explained in conversations how God informed their daily practice and gave them hope. Spirituality was elusive but undeniably present. It was a spirituality that could be embraced by all people and a religious expression. It was noted that peoples of various theologies, religions, and philosophies made up the membership of Padres Unidos, including atheists and theists.

To uncover the role of spirituality within the Padres' organization, Chapman researchers needed to unlearn their secular bias. They needed to investigate other codes, principles, and values that were core to the organization's identity. Looking beyond one's discipline requires more than a rhetorical exercise, it demands humility, an acknowledgement of what one does not know and an understanding that one has much to learn. "Spirit phobia" (Keating, 2008) made us, as well as other scholars outside the theological discipline, hesitant to speak of spirituality. In recent years, however, "conversations on spirituality have expanded its traditional borders, and have become broader and more eclectic" (Kirylo & Boyd, 2017, pp. xviii–xix). "Freire admitted he was reticent to discuss it (spirituality) publicly" (Boyd, 2012, p. 760).

Discovering something that was new, researchers tried to learn more. We learned that spirituality can take on many different meanings and can also be en*acted* in just as many ways. This variance can depend on one's underlying theology. The role that action plays in theology varies depending on the religious tradition. Researching Paulo Freire's early works in liberation theology and critical spirituality (Boyd, 2012; Dantley, 2003; Kirylo & Boyd, 2017; McLaren, 2015) helped us identify an intersection between Jesuit theology and critical theory that had not be prominent in current critical pedagogy literature. Jesuit tradition focused on promoting community action with groups who were in greatest need (Pace & Merys, 2016). As a consequence of their theology, the Jesuits emphasize action as an extension of their doctrinal beliefs (Gannett & Brereton, 2016). During the 1960s, a beacon call to action was announced during the Second Vatican Council (Vatican II) which encouraged Catholics to actively participate in their communities (Call to Action, 2017).

Unlearning and relearning are critical dispositions in research and partnership relationships. Communities are unique and vibrant, living organisms whose fullness cannot be reduced to scientific metrics. While we familiarized Padres Unidos with the philosophy of Paulo Freire and critical pedagogy, Padres Unidos helped Chapman researchers rediscover Freire by connecting us to his earlier spiritual Jesuit foundation. They helped us see the spiritual roots of Freire's social justice orientation and opened our eyes to see things more broadly.

As community and university partners, there are realities that we can miss in each other if we aren't open to the unexpected. The reality of another can shed light upon our own reality. Not every community is spiritual. Spirituality just happened to be the novel revelation we came upon, one which drew us closer to each other as partners. The lesson we learned was that true partnership cannot take place until we stand hospitably to welcome seemingly incommunicable aspects while opening ourselves in return. When we do this, partnerships bloom like flowers along the road to an unforeseen future.

LET'S CHAT
CAFECITO II (Individual or Dialogue)

Think about a time when you learned something that made you change the way you did things?

Did that new learning cause you discomfort?

Did you adapt to this new learning or reject it? Why?

Activity

Take some time to think about all the things that make your family or group of friends unique. Imagine that someone was going to write about them tomorrow. What are some aspects that someone might not grasp by looking from the outside? Do we carry biases when we look at the world? How might you prepare yourself to discover the unexpected in someone else? How do you prepare yourself to discover the unexpected in you?

References

Boyd, D. (2012). The critical spirituality of Paulo Freire. *International Journal of Lifelong Education, 31*(6), 759-778. doi:10.1080/02601370.2012.723051

Call to Action. (2017). History. http://cta-usa.org/history/

Dantley, M. (2003). Critical spirituality: Enhancing transformative leadership through critical theory and african-American prophetic spirituality. *International Journal of Leadership in Education, 6*(1), 3-17.

Freire, P. (2004). *Pedegogy of the oppressed.* New York, NY: Continuum.

Gannett, C., & Brereton, J. C. (2016). Introduction: The Jesuits and rhetorical studies - looking backward, moving forward. In C. Gannett & J. C. Brereton (Eds.), *Traditions of eloquence: The Jesuits and modern rhetorical studies.* New York NY: Fordham University Press.

Gies, E. (2017). The meaning of lichen: How a self-taught naturalist unearthed hidden symbioses in the wilds of british columbia - and helped to overturn 150 years of accepted scientific wisdom. *Scientific American,* 53-59. http://ericagies.com/write/the-meaning-of-lichen-scientific-american/

Keating, A. (2008). "I'm a citizen of the universe": Gloria Anzaldua's spiritual activism as catalyst for social change. *Feminist Studies, 34*(1/2), 54-69.

Kirylo, J. D., & Boyd, D. (2017). *Paulo Freire: His faith, spirituality, and theology.* Rotterdam, The Netherlands: Sense Publishers.

McLaren, P. (2015). *Pedagogy of insurrection: From resurrection to revolution.* New York, NY: Peter Lang Publishing.

Pace, T., & Merys, G. M. (2016). Paulo Freire and the Jesuit tradition: Jesuit rhetoric and freirean pedagogy In C. Gannett & J. C. Brereton (Eds.), *Traditions of eloquence: The Jesuits and modern rhetorical studies.* New York NY: Fordham University Press.

Dear Mom,

One of my army buddies was
recently rescued from an
explosion. He pulled through
the trauma but lost his legs and

to

Story: The Man Who Returned from War

At the end of a beautiful street in a beautiful neighborhood lived the perfect, beautiful family. They were model citizens, held in high esteem by all. When their eldest son turned eighteen, he decided to enter the army. It was the perfect thing to do.

One day, the mother received a letter from her son while he was away. It read, "Dear Mom, One of my army buddies was recently rescued from an explosion. He pulled through the trauma but lost his legs and arms in the process. As a friend, I am very concerned for him. He's not going to be able to take care of himself. Would you and Dad take care of him? Love, your son." The mom wrote back, "Dear Son, You have such a big, beautiful heart! Your father and I have so many things to do. Our involvement in our organizations and clubs make it hard for us to care for him. He needs a much higher level of care than we can offer. We better not take him in. Maybe you could place him in a home where he can be taken better care of. Love, your Mom."

Soon after that, the parents ceased getting mail from their son. They became very concerned. They didn't know if he was alive. As they began to seek answers about his disappearance, they discovered that he was in a convalescent home across the state. Without hesitation, they packed their bags and drove to see him.

Upon opening the door to his room, the parents saw their son. He had neither arms nor legs. Crying, the mom asked, "Why you didn't come home? We would have taken care of you!" The son looked intently at his parents, saying, "I did not want to be a burden to you. I have no legs, no arms, I'm crippled! I didn't want to interfere in your life."

LET'S CHAT
CAFECITO I (Individual or Dialogue)

Is this story challenging? If so, how?

Can you think of ethical dilemmas like this one in your life?

How did you distinguish in these dilemmas a "bad" decision from a "good" decision?

What is the reasoning for your answer?

Discussion

The moral of the parable which opens this chapter is clear: Act rightly toward others, no matter who they are. Serving the needs of a young man in distress was presented to these parents by their son as a moral option. By placing other priorities first, the parents acted in a way that neglected another for the sake of maintaining the status quo of their lives. The result of this act was the isolation of their son and the disintegration of the bonds of family. Like these parents, we too are faced with ethical choices, often without fully knowing the consequence of our choices. Scholar David Leigh (2016) explains that when people are faced with ethical or moral uncertainty, the best that they can do is to choose from an array of options with the goal of consistently applying ethical goals. How do we make such choices? What are the guiding principles of our daily actions? These are the questions of ethics.

As partners, we have taken reflective pauses in our research and dialogues to understand what ethics frame the ways that we interact with the world, both alone and as partners. In these discussions, it was discovered that we agreed on many of the most basic tenants about what it looks like to be a good person. This included our mutual understandings about what it meant to be benevolent partners in the research and writing process. The source of the commonly held assumptions about ethical behavior as community and university partners were not always the same. For some, ethics derived from reflections on the nature of democracy and its consequent mandates on right living. For others, ethics derived from spiritual beliefs about the human person and the world itself. Drawing on our knowledge and experience of ethics from these two sources, we learned to understand the ethics of partnership in a fuller way. What developed is what we termed relational ethics.

Democracy is an ethical concept that, by its very nature, embraces all aspects of social life. Popularly, democracy is often understood in terms of procedure, essentially linking democracy with the political procedure of voting and electing representatives (Critchley, 2001). However, linking democracy only to political procedure obscures other important aspects of a holistic democratic life, including the social and economic (Niemi, 2011). *True democracy* is more than procedural and urges us to orient and unify social, political, and economic aspects of our lives towards the goal of promoting equality and freedom (Niemi, 2011). In action, valuing of democratic practices by recognizing their primacy in achieving ethical goals is known as the *prefigurative tradition*. Prefigurative democracy is a process-oriented model for social transformation which regards *right* action and *right* goals as mutually defined. You must *do* good in order to move toward good ends. If an organization chooses to support a democracy (economically, socially, and politically), then they would engage in democratic actions.

Spiritually, ethics imply a morality that holds the *Other* as sacred. In the Jesuit tradition, community action is integral to spiritual fulfillment. As Gannett and Brereton (2016) explained, the Jesuits fostered ministries of the world, as opposed to the "more contemplative, older Catholic orders…which had tended to establish their monasteries at rural sites and to restrict their engagements with the larger world" (Section 2, para. 7). Gannett and Brereton (2016) explained further that Jesuits were much more civically engaged, often seeking spaces that were the center of political power and public influence. The Jesuits support their community-centered practice through the process of discernment. The Jesuit rhetorical practice of discernment links action with goals, or specifically with *good* action with *good* goals. In Grogan and Shakeshaft's (2011) study, women in educational leadership attributed spirituality in the form of hope that inspired them to push forward in conflictual and difficult situations. The ethical weight of discernment, or its bend to do the right thing, carries a similar action/goal orientation as the prefigurative tradition. Within both frames, morality and the goal of service to others are the ever-present drivers of action in the day-to-day process of the work.

Drawing from the wells of both democratic and spiritual reflection, we realized that our partnership ethics could be seen in truly *relational* terms. Describing the partnership as solely democratic is unfinished and incomplete because it was existential spirituality that gave us hope and compassion that deepened our democratic commitments and caused us to focus intently on how we should act toward one another. It was a combination of prophetic Christian thought and practice with democratic critical consciousness and praxis merging together with a similar moral view — to respect and dignify each individual — as we struggle *together* to address social and economic inequality. Partnership requires that we interact ethically with others and acknowledge our *relational being*. The study of *being* (known as ontology in philosophy) understands that from our earliest days we become who we are because of the people around us. The perspective has the consequence of establishing a deep, inextricable link between ourselves and others. Martin Buber (1970), a twentieth-century philosopher, explained that such a deep relationship establishes an ongoing moral responsibility to those around us. Therefore, as an ethical view, a *relational ethic* considers a person holistically, with equal emphasis to all aspects of our humanity, including our political, social, economic, and spiritual selves. This has consequences for how we consider ethics in our social as well as our spiritual lives.

The Chapman University and Padres Unidos research team helped strengthen their organizations' partnership by utilizing this *relational* ethic. Perhaps most central to the ethics of partnership was the practice of dialogue. Dialogue with others was a means to democratic engagement and spiritual practice. This is particularly true when the Other of our dialogue is seen as our equal and co-participant in the ethical work of bringing about a better future. Both organizations utilized dialogue in their teaching practices, which helped center the curriculum around the participants themselves. Chapman University members often utilize teaching practices based around Paulo Freire's cultural circles to encourage equitable participation. Similarly, Padres Unidos utilized *circles of love* (cultural circles) in their teaching spaces. As Paloma, a Padres Unidos community worker, described the circles of love, they "provide a safe space to allow others to be vulnerable. A safe and friendly place that give people the opportunity to grow." The ethic translates organizationally where both partners tend to comport to flat-organizational structures that limit inherent power structures and promote equitable participation. Finally, as service providers in the community, Padres Unidos members regard the families as constituents in their own process, known as *walking with them*, which depicts a service model that acknowledges an individual's needs and desires rather than prescribing solutions.

The partnership resulting from the relational approach helped establish novel models for community university partnerships. The relational ethic was suggestive of community university partnerships that are not defined in binaries, but, holistically, as integrated units. When the frame is taken to its logical extent, the vision for community university partnerships should be defined not only as *mutual* interest, but as a shared participation in doing and seeking good. By understanding what brought us to the common understanding of ethics, each of our own ethical frames became better informed. Seeing what it meant to do good was a way for us to contemplate what part the good of others plays in our own lives.

LET'S CHAT
CAFECITO II (Individual or Dialogue)

What are the ethics that you bring into your relationships with others socially or in the workplace? What is your ethical belief system based upon? Faith? Politics? Family traditions?

Many businesses and organizations use the term *core values* to describe the ethics that underscore their work. Can you tell by the way businesses and organizations operate, what are their core values?

Activity

In order to avoid ethical missteps and oversights, we found that identifying with political clarity the deliberate democratic principles that were fundamental to our partnership helped us navigate through difficult times. Processes of discernment also guided us when we lost our way. For example, reminding ourselves who we are, what we stand for, and not allowing other tangentially related initiatives to redirect our purpose prove to be morally stabilizing.

Make a list of the core values (ethical/moral principles) that inform and hold true in your clubs or organizations. What do you observe when the organization is in crisis? How does the organization navigate through troubled waters? Does the organization work in concert or contradiction to its core values? What happens? What recommendations would you offer?

References

Buber, M. (1970). *I and thou*. New York, NY: Charles Scribner's Sons.

Critchley, P. (2001). *Marx, reason, and freedom: Communism, rational freedom and socialised humanity*. Manchester Metropolitan University.

David Leigh, S. J. (2016). The changing practice of liberal education and rhetoric in Jesuit education, 1600– 2000 In C. Gannett & J. C. Brereton (Eds.), *Traditions of eloquence: The Jesuits and modern rhetorical studies*. New York, NY: Fordham University Press.

Gannett, C., & Brereton, J. C. (2016). Introduction: The Jesuits and rhetorical studies - looking backward, moving forward. In C. Gannett & J. C. Brereton (Eds.), *Traditions of eloquence: The Jesuits and modern rhetorical studies*. New York NY: Fordham University Press.

Niemi, W. L. (2011). Karl Marx's sociological theory of democracy: Civil society and political rights. *The Social Science Journal, 48,* 39-51.

TRANSFORMATION & HOPE

Story: The Parable of Eagles Who Live for Thirty Years

It is believed that, while most eagles only live for fifteen years, there are some who live to the age of thirty. The doubling of the lifespan is said to be a result of a very special practice. Most other eagles die at the age of fifteen as a result of the dulling and aging of their claws, beaks, and feathers. But for the thirty-year-old eagles, things are different.

When these eagles are fifteen, they recognize their weakened condition and fly up to the tallest mountain. First, they strip off their claws, making themselves unable to defend themselves. When new claws grow in, they then use these to scratch off their aged beak so that a fresh one may take its place. Finally, they use this beak to pluck out all their feathers to allow new ones to grow in. Once that process is finished, they return to their home to live for fifteen more years.

Even though this is a myth, it tells us a truth about human life. We start life with pristine beaks, claws, and feathers. But due to poor choices and unfortunate events in life, our beaks, claws, and feathers become worn. At this point, it is good for us to take stock of who we are and what we have. If we fail to look at ourselves and really evaluate every part of our lives, then we start dying inside. We might miss the chance to become the person that we were meant to be.

There are people who live one hundred years but are not happy inside. They don't enjoy life, dissatisfied with the world they have created. It's ugly. That's why we must take this journey of re-evaluating ourselves and our lives. We must get rid of those things that are holding us back, recognizing that our past is truly behind us.

We must come to understand that we are no longer in that former time. Like the transformed eagles, we give ourselves the gift of regeneration and begin life anew.

LET'S CHAT
CAFECITO I (Individual or Dialogue)

How do you renew yourself?

How did you deal with that situation?

Can you think of a time when your past experiences got in the way of you moving forward?

What value does self-reflection provide to you personally? At school? In the workplace? In community organizations?

Discussion

The parable of the eagle who lives for thirty years is one of the treasured stories used by Padres Unidos to demonstrate the value of transformation. As with all metaphoric teachings, this story allows for the listener to discover various layers of meaning. The subsequent exposition on the story's moral also invites the listener to apply the idea of transformation to themselves in individual ways. No doubt, each person will walk away with their own convictions about what transformation will mean in their lives.

There are almost as many theories and ideas about transformation as there are persons who use the word. So, dear reader, before we go any further into this chapter, we would like to ask you some of the same questions that plagued us in understanding this concept. By so doing, we hope that you will think *with us* about the complex process of becoming something new. How do you define transformation? Is it a noun or a verb? How do you know it when you see or experience it? We know that evaluators and researchers want to measure it as a marker of change. Is transformation any change or change of a certain kind? Is transformation a concrete reality, as when one's cellular makeup is altered in an unretractable way? Is it an experience, like when one first discovers the Big Dipper in the sky, forever altering one's perception of a certain reality? Is it relational, developing over time between persons? Is it an alteration in social constructions? Must it be marked by physical manifestations of change? Thinking through these questions might reveal that you hold in yourself multiple definitions of transformation. It is a complex concept.

Padres Unidos members recognized transformation through their connection to each other. As Rafaela, a senior Padres Unidos member, explained, "Many times, even when we see ourselves in the mirror every day, we can't visualize all that we have grown…in the spiritual way and the personal way in which we see things, until we see it reflected in someone else or someone reflects it back to us."

Her reflection challenges an individualistic idea of change. Rafaela's mirror metaphor reminds us of the significant role that our peers, partners, and community members play in helping us define who we are and what our purpose is as students, organizers, or community members.

Padres Unidos' understanding of transformation is demonstrated in the organization's work of helping individuals overcome obstacles as a community. Program organizer Patty Meza conveys that students bring a multitude of experiences to the program. These students come from various countries and societies. Some individuals come facing coercion and violence in their daily lives. For example, some families have come from abusive families; others, from war-ravaged countries. These histories have made them unsure of their ability to be a beneficial force in the lives of their families. What these students face can feel insurmountable.

Despite the challenges that they bring to the program, many students end classes with Padres reporting positive feelings of transformation. When describing how the program was transformative for her, one Padres student used the metaphor of Hello Kitty, "When I first started the program, I had no mouth, no voice. Now at the end of the program, I have a toolkit of resources to empower myself." Another student revealed she started out as a rough, unpolished rock that has changed into a luminous, multifaceted diamond. Finally, a veteran of the program declared that her time with Padres changed her life so profoundly that she wanted to become a trainer and a role model for others. "I want to be a little pencil to help others write a new story for their lives."

As close-working partners, Chapman University researchers defined transformation similarly to Padres Unidos. Chapman researchers reflected on ethicist Martin Buber's (1970) relational philosophy, which considers our loved ones, partners, and colleagues as indispensable factors in coming to understand ourselves. This was philosophically similar to Rafaela's mirror metaphor. In their own classrooms, the Chapman partners sought to create transformative learning environments. They engaged in curricula which stimulated identity development, empowerment, self-esteem, and the development of role models. Critical educator Antonia Darder (2014) explains that transformative learning can occur when "teachers create conditions for students to critically question, deconstruct and recreate knowledge without repercussions or reprisals, in ways that enhance their sense of ethical responsibility to self and community" (p. 87). Therefore, transformation is a social experience that mutually effects the individual and society in relation to each other.

For us, transformation began with the intentional encounter of a sustained partnership. Padres Unidos and Chapman University researchers came to define their partnership as a kind of relationship. This meant that we accommodated one another and made strategic adjustments in the pursuit of ensuring that the partnership was equitable. When considering the partnership in relational terms, change is constantly occurring. This change can be positive or negative, depending on the ways that we choose to relate to one another. Further, as a consequence of understanding change in these terms, *hope* can be a considerable driving force in promoting positive change. Within the partnership, Padres Unidos and Chapman University members experienced positive transformation driven by a deep, shared feeling of *hope*.

Transformation in our partnership was fueled by hope. Shor and Freire (1987) noted that "hope is the relationship between denouncing the present and announcing the future" in which we "anticipate tomorrow by dreaming today" (Shor & Freire, 1987, p. 187, as cited in Roberts, 2015, p. 382). It is "more than just an exercise in wishful thinking, it is a political and moral imperative…that represents a refusal to accept the world the way it is" (Lake & Kress, 2017, pp. 70–71). As partners, we were committed to the vision of a world in which values like equity and democracy might dictate a better future for all. In light of this hope, we opened ourselves up to a relationship that could challenge and transform us. Therefore, for the partners, hope which led to transformation meant working together between theoretical visions and concrete actions geared toward creating a better world (Roberts, 2015). We believed each other to be the mirror that reflected our inner change as our relationship grew. As with all genuine hope, we acknowledge no foreseeable limit to the possibilities of transformation. Each change reveals new potentials for ourselves and the world around us.

LET'S CHAT
CAFECITO II (Individual or Dialogue)

How would you prepare yourself to be open to transformation?

How is hope tacitly or explicitly expressed in an organization to which you belong?

How is hope (the space between what is and what could be) a key component of transformation for yourself and the organization of which you belong?

Activity

In demonstrating the value of the role of self-reflection and introspection in the life of a project or organization, develop three good questions that would help your organization conduct a reflective assessment of its strengths and weaknesses. Compare your questions with your partner's and analyze the merits of the questions.

References

Buber, M. (1970). *I and thou*. New York, NY: Charles Scribner's Sons.

Darder, A. (2014). *Freire and education:* Routledge.

Lake, R., & Kress, T. (2017). Mamma don't put that blue guitar in a museum: Greene and Freire's duet of radical hope in hopeless times. *Review of Education, Pedagogy, and Cultural Studies, 39*(1), 60-75.

Roberts, P. (2015). Paulo Freire and utopian education. *Review of Education, Pedagogy, and Cultural Studies, 37*(5), 376-392. doi: 10.1080/10714413.2015.1091256

Shor, I., & Freire, P. (1987). *A pedagogy for liberation: Dialogues on transforming education* (Kindle ed.): Bergin & Garvey Publishers.

SCHOLARLY ACTIVIST

Story: *The Piano*

Padre Miguel was the proud pastor of a church in a small town in Mexico. A few years ago, he bought a beautifully handcrafted piano for his church. It made the most enchanting sounds during Mass. People came from towns and cities across the country to spend their Sunday listening to the music of the piano and enjoying the food that local vendors sold in the streets. It was a blessing to the little impoverished pueblo.

One morning, the piano fell silent. Padre Miguel felt responsible to fix it. He tried but was unable to make the instrument play. He invited the most knowledgeable experts from Germany to come and repair the piano. None were able to return its sound. One day, Gio, the parish custodian, asked the priest if he could try to fix the piano. Padre Miguel scoffed, "Every expert has tried already. You think you can do better than them?" Gio shook his head yes. The priest prayed and thought he ought to give the custodian a chance and see what he could do.

Gio took the entire piano apart into many little pieces. Townspeople passing through the sanctuary of the church were shocked. Many started to shout at the custodian and threatened him for destroying the instrument. Hearing this, Padre Miguel came into the church to see what was wrong. Even though he too was shocked by the sight of the piano in so many parts, the priest silenced the crowd: "Let him be, he is doing his work!" He moved the people out of the sanctuary and closed the church doors, giving Gio his space.

By the end of the day, familiar enchanting melodies came from the sanctuary. They all rushed in the church with the priest to see Gio playing the piano. "How did you know what to do?" asked Padre Miguel. Gio smiled, "Well, Padre, I know this piano very well. I built it, and so, I knew what was wrong. I just needed to be given a chance to fix it."

LET'S CHAT
CAFECITO I (Individual or Dialogue)

Like Father Miguel, have you ever felt you were responsible to fix an issue because of your familiarity in a situation?

Who do you typically ask for help when something goes wrong?

Have you ever given someone a chance to help you who surprised you by their expertise?

Discussion

In our opening story, the parish priest learned an important lesson. His role in the small town was significant since he was a leader and sage. People looked to him for guidance. When things went wrong, he felt he was responsible for having the answer. He turned to his own expertise and those of learned experts to solve the community's problems. But, in the end, he discovered that the wisdom to change the fortune of the town must come from the town itself. When he stepped back and honored the custodian's wisdom, even when he was skeptical, he learned a new kind of leadership. One can only imagine how his perception of his expert role changed into one of "spiritual facilitator," honoring the gifts of his congregation.

Like priests, academic scholars are seen as experts whose position in society is substantiated by ritual practices and specialized knowledge. As scholars, they can sense a need to have solutions to all of the problems of the world. However, Paulo Freire (1984) contends that scholars need to completely reinvent themselves and revolutionize their perspectives so that they can truly serve the community. Perhaps his insistence on this reinvention is derived from his work in liberation theology. It is a spiritual tradition which prioritizes the interests and the needs of the most downtrodden in society (Kirylo & Boyd, 2017). Drawing from his deep theological roots, Freire (1984) explains that the scholar "must 'die' in order to be reborn through and with the oppressed" (p. 524). Known as the Easter experience, Boyd (2017) contends that the inner reinvention of the scholar reflects an ongoing process of seeking to be in solidarity with the poor.

Chapman University and Padres Unidos partners recognized that they came to the table of research from two sides of a historical divide between academics and local community members. It was a division that needed to be overcome. Each partner entered a transformative journey of self-reflection and critical soul-searching about their place and role in society. From this came the emergence of a "we" that would mark the unique nature of this community university partnership. Collectively, we imbued our research practices with an ethic of respect for our relationship. The maintenance of the "we" in the relationship defines the very core of our work. Thus, our journeys led us to become scholarly activists and organic intellectuals in communion with each other.

We invite you to ponder with us some critical questions. They are queries that we found ourselves asking throughout the partnership. Our answers to these questions have defined our ethical and philosophical parameters, leading us into a more vibrant partnership.

What should our stance be when entering our work?

In answering this, we reflect on a quote of Freire (1998): "Those who come from 'another world' to the world of people who do so not as invaders. They do not come to <u>teach</u> or to <u>transmit</u> or to give anything, but rather to learn, with the people, about the people's world" (p. 180). Freire's words remind us that an outsider (or researcher) must come first to learn. Qualitative research, such as the work of our partnership, is an invitation to enter an inner sanctum of human testimonies where people make sense of the world. Therefore, we need to come with reverence, respect and humility.

What right do we have to study the Other?

Chapman University partners understood themselves to be members of an expanding group of researchers who are committed to decolonizing and humanizing research. As such, our goal is to respect the humanity of the people who invite us into their worlds (Paris & Winn, 2014). This respect mandates that we interrogate ourselves, asking, "What right do we have to study others? Who are we? What biases, experiences, skills or resources do we bring to the research? What are our expectations and research goals? Do they match those of our participants?"

Prior to entering the field of research, Chapman students are asked, in their coursework, to engage in subjectivity activities such as writing autobiographical essays, creating poetry, constructing of ya-ya boxes (collaged boxes depicting identity with visual images) (Janesick, 2004), assembling quilts, and/or choreographing performances. These activities encourage reflection that reveals the "emotional and intellectual baggage" that researchers often bring into research settings (Behar, 1996, p. 8). These exercises help researchers recognize how "they are both insiders and outsiders in relation to topic, setting and participants" (Johnson, 2017, p. 60). When coupled with a commitment to respect, the discovery of one's subjectivity dictates how one can ethically enter into research with others.

How does one gain entry?

How does one earn trust and credibility? By what means do we ethically encroach on the mental landscape of others while proving ourselves trustworthy? How do we respectfully conduct and disseminate research? Qualitative research is conducted within a social context. Here, human beings gift their stories, feelings, and activities. They are bearers of genuine knowledge. As every context is unique, we realize that we must re-evaluate what constitutes an ethical engagement within each culture. There is no perfect formula, only this critical question: What are the rituals of encounter in any given community?

What do we know that prevents us from learning more?

In asking this question, we found ourselves pondering the depth of these poetic lines by Lamott (1995):

Why does the bird sing?
The bird sings not because she has a statement but because she has a song (p. 181).

Because university researchers are prone to analysis, we are more likely to be attuned to the bird's statement. But what must we, as scholars, do to hear the song? Our world of words often fosters a detached intellectualism that gets in the way of human relationships and other forms of literacy. By liberating ourselves from the tyranny of written words, we prepared ourselves for more personable ways of learning and understanding each other in the partnership. This freedom allowed us to acknowledge the "somebodiness of each individual in that community" (Kirylo & Boyd, 2017, p. 29).

What does it mean to be community-based researchers?

Johnson's (2017) work enumerates the many roles and stances of the community-based qualitative researcher: Teachers and Facilitators, Ambassadors and Allies, Advocates and Activists. They are also described as boundary spanners (Reardon & Leonard, 2017), individuals that fluidly cross the traditional divide between university and community, increasing resources and opportunities. Some of these roles prove to be more challenging than others because "faculty are trained to think as intellectuals, not as organizers" (Saltmarsh & Hartley, 2011, p. 9).

Saltmarsh and Hartley (2011) invite those in higher education to consider civic engagement through the lens of a larger democratic project. From this perspective, the researchers are required to interact "with other knowledge production outside the university for the creation of new problem-solving knowledge through a multidirectional flow of knowledge and expertise" (p. 21). This interaction helps universities to reframe traditional notions of expertise. University researchers begin to re-conceptualize the relationship between themselves and communities. "Without a democratic purpose, engagement becomes reduced to a public relations function…" (p. 18). Our democratic goal in the partnership is simple: Together, we work to "expand the capacity of participants to make change in their own lives and communities" (Dyrness, 2011, p. 201). Thus, community-based means more than locality, it means repositioning research to be *with* and *for* communities.

What comes from a partnership that embraces this ethic?

Our answer to this question could only be conjecture at the outset of our project. When researchers move from authoritative figures to fellow-sojourners in the process of discovery, one cannot know the end result. Three years of relationship-building preceded research in this partnership. Our ethical stance mandated that we earned the right to become "we." Reverence for the other with accompanying ethical action paved the way. The result has been a beautiful and unique relational unity, one which is marked by collective transformation. What it means to be a researcher and also what it means to be a member of a community merged into a vibrant, knowledge bearing relationship.

What characteristic distinguishes a scholarly activist?

As we have noted, the history and present reality of community and university relations are all too often marked by injustice and inequality. Many traditional forms of academic research are characterized by dehumanizing practices, which assert the superiority of university scholars over the communities they research (Smith, 1999). One cannot become a scholarly activist without acknowledging and disavowing the present construct of power (Freire, 1984). While the individual scholar may not be able to change society and systemic inequality alone, he or she can choose to refuse to take advantage of undue and oppressive privileges afforded him by this system. Acting in this way is what we have come to term "intellectual modesty." Scholarly activists ought to step back, make room, and advocate for voices and ways of knowing which are often silenced. This intellectual modesty, more importantly, makes possible the development of authentic relationships as researchers forego the myth of exceptionality for a reality of equity.

LET'S CHAT
CAFECITO II (Individual or Dialogue)

As a scholarly activist, what are your research goals?

How will your goals benefit the academy?
The community?

What are your partnering community's past experiences with university researchers?

How will you prepare yourself to enter into your partnering community?

Activity

Conduct a self-inventory of the knowledge, skills, talents, and experiences you bring to the community. What biases and privileges do you bring as well? How are you both an insider and an outsider with respect to the topic, participants, or settings?

References

Behar, R. (1996). *The vulnerable observer: Anthropology that breaks your heart*. Boston, MA: Beacon Press.

Boyd, D. (2017). The Easter experience: Conversion to the people. In J. D. Kirylo & D. Boyd (Eds.), *Paulo Freire: His faith, spirituality, and theology*. Rotterdam, The Netherlands: Sense Publishers.

Dyrness, A. (2011). *Mothers united: An immigrant struggle for socially just education*. Minneapolis, MN: University of Minnesota Press.

Freire, P. (1984). Education, liberation, and the church. *Religious Education, 79*(4), 524-545.

Freire, P. (2010). *Pedagogy of the oppressed*. NY: Continuum.

Janesick, V. (2004). *Stretching exercises for qualitative researchers*. New York, NY: Sage.

Johnson, L. R. (2017). *Community-based qualitative research*. New York, NY: Sage.

Kirylo, J. D., & Boyd, D. (2017). *Paulo Freire: His faith, spirituality, and theology*. Rotterdam, The Netherlands: Sense Publishers.

Lamont, A. (1995). *Bird by bird: Some instructions about writing and life*. New York, NY: Anchor Books.

Paris, D., & Winn, M. (2014). *Humanizing research: Decolonizing qualitative inquiry with youth and communities*. SAGE Publications: Los Angeles, CA.

Reardon, R. M., & Leonard, J. (2017). *Exploring the community impact of research-practice partnerships in education*. Charlotte, NC: IAP.

Saltmarsh, J., & Hartley, M. (2011). *To serve a larger purpose": Engagement for democracy and the transformation of higher education*. Temple University Press: Philadelphia, PA.

Smith, L. T. (1999). *Decolonizing methodologies: Research and indigenous peoples*. Zed Books Ltd.: London, UK.

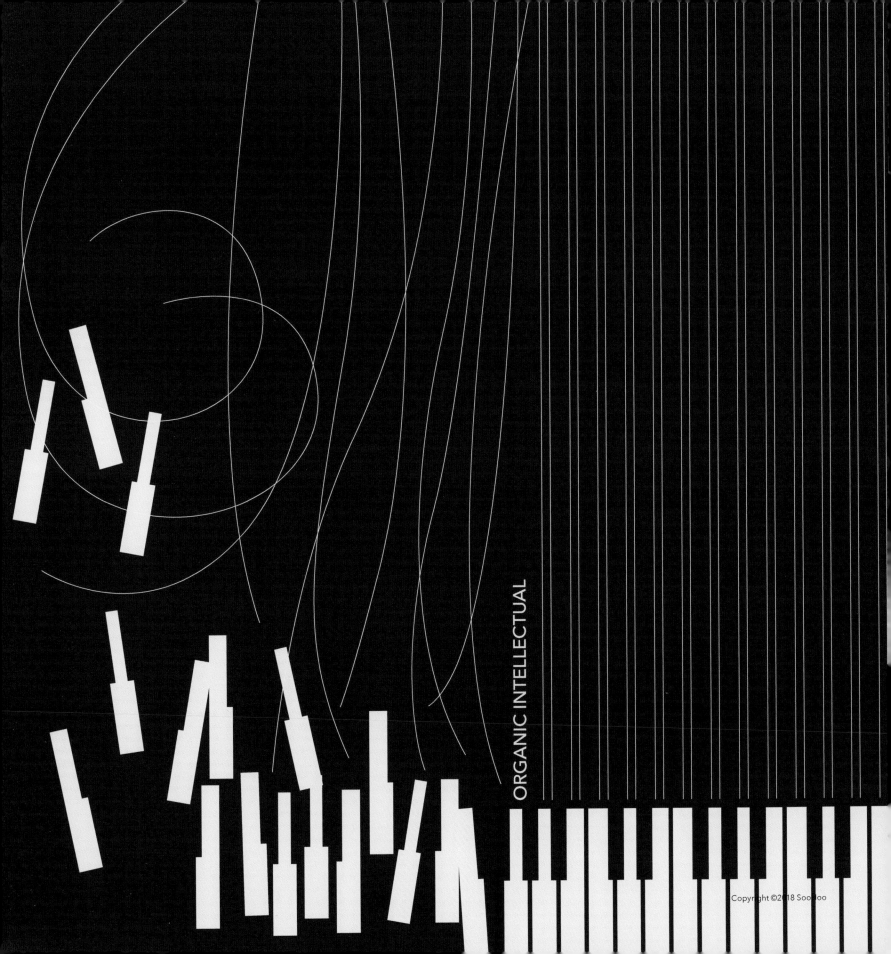

ORGANIC INTELLECTUAL

Story: The Piano

Gio always considered himself a simple man. He lived most of his life in a poor little town in Mexico. When he was twenty, he left his little town for Guadalajara. There he got a job with a piano maker, Maestro Rafael, and spent several years assisting him. Gio even had the chance to build a piano of his own and signed its leg. It was magnificent. But Gio felt very disconnected from his home and the people. So, he gave up the trade to return to his pueblo.

Many years later, the parish got a priest named Padre Miguel. He hired Gio as his custodian. The priest began to beautify the church and bought a new piano to fill it with music. When the instrument arrived, Gio noticed his own name signed on its leg. He said nothing.

The piano made the most enchanting sounds, bringing people from across Mexico. They spent their Sundays in Mass listening to the piano and spending their money at the vendors. This was a blessing to the poor town. That is, until the piano fell silent and refused to play. Padre Miguel tried to repair the instrument himself. He even brought experts in from Germany to try to fix it. Nothing worked. So, people stopped visiting the town.

Gio knew what was wrong, even though he did not want to admit it. He asked permission to try to fix the piano. Padre Miguel was confused but allowed him to try. Gio disassembled the entire instrument into its smallest parts, alarming on-lookers. Padre Miguel moved an angry crowd out of the church, leaving Gio to work in the church alone. When the sanctuary was silent, he began to speak to the parts of the piano saying: "Little pieces, I first brought you together out of pride. But pride does not make beautiful music forever. Today I want you to know I put you back together out of love. You will be a piano of love for all the people in this pueblo. Your music will bring them blessings." Silently, he rebuilt the instrument.

That night, Gio started playing the piano. Its music was so beautiful that it brought all the people into the church. Gio saw that the blessing of the piano was not that it brought strangers to the town, but that it brought the community together and gave them purpose.

LET'S CHAT
CAFECITO I (Individual or Dialogue)

Who do you consider to be your community? Where do you find yourself most at home?

Is there a time that you had a gift that your community needed you to share?

Have you ever been hesitant to step up to do something because you did not want to be the center of attention?

Discussion

Gio's moving confidence and courage to step up helped bring the community together again. While restoring an integral aspect of the community's social life, Gio's competence challenged popular assumptions about a janitor's role in his community. Similarly, Padres Unidos' approach to community building relies on the ability of individual members to grow in their personal capacities with their friends and families to better their communities. Padres Unidos believes this wisdom is inherent in all the members of the local community with whom they work. For some, it is very apparent, while in others this latent wisdom is waiting to be actualized in their personal lives. The organization's commitment to strengthening the local community is directly tied to its work in realizing the potential of each individual. Programs are geared toward helping people to grow in their personal relational capacities with their friends and families. This, in turn, leads members of Padres to better their communities. Camencita describes the phenomena at a personal level, where she pays-forward the opportunity that she was given by working in the community. Further, during the process of growth, many members of the organization realize their affinity for community work and how they have gained a deep sense of meaning from that work. As a result, personal growth becomes nearly indistinguishable from family or community growth, as the deep bonds foster mutual growth and the members see themselves as an integral part of the community.

Padres Unidos members become an integral part of the community through their ability to speak up for their community. This is significant as community knowledge is sometimes devalued, and all too discredited in public arenas where, as Ludwig (2017) notes, local knowledge is sometimes understood to lack the "epistemic resources" necessary to explain complex phenomena (p. 4705). Padres Unidos helps community members to bring their values first into safe communal spaces and, later, to public spaces where community members are sometimes barred. The natural development of community knowledge and its delivery to broader society recall Gramsci's notion (Zimmerman, 2017) of the organic intellectual that encourages the community member to *step up* and demand of society a place at the table.

Padres Unidos helps develop organic intellectuals through a family-centered, community-focused approach where individuals learn to develop alongside their peers, colleagues, friends, and family. Basilia, a community worker, explained her close work with other community members:

> *I have enriched myself with teachings that I am always going to have with me to help others as they have helped me... This change in my life has been a great change, a positive and grand personal change for me and also to help the community.*

The community members ability to navigate the various institutions and structures requires a unique perspective as they bring resources back to the community. The struggle that organic intellectuals face in the decision to maintain their values as community members while also striving to be included in broader social, political, and economic discussions reminds us of W.E.B. Du Bois, who struggled during the fight for Black liberation (Butler, 2006). Butler (2006) describes how Du Bois described his internal conflict in terms of "double-consciousness" where he acknowledged the struggle to simultaneously maintain Black identity in the face of racism while also moving toward becoming a part of the larger "American" community (p. 177). Put simply, Du Bois hoped to have both, to be both Black and to be American, so that he could "be a co-worker in the kingdom of culture" (Butler, 2006, p. 177). In a similar bind, organic intellectuals today struggle to maintain their identity and affiliation with their community while also stepping into roles that can help bring resources to their community.

This struggle is part and parcel of the community's members belief in Incarnating Wisdom, of putting flesh onto their structure of self and community development. If the mark of an ethical academic in response to the inequity which exists between universities and communities is "epistemological modesty," then there is likewise a complementary attribute demonstrated in the life of the organic intellectual. While community organizations, such as Padres Unidos, believe that each person holds within herself or himself particular gifts and insights which can build up others, it is similarly attested that most people hold these gifts and insights in unrealized potential. This wisdom, which is inherent to the community, must be freely shared and lived. It serves no purpose while untapped. Organic intellectuals move beyond reductionist academic definitions of knowledge to embrace a wider understanding of fruitful intelligence. When putting the skills and knowledge they learned from their community to the use of building up that same community, organic intellectuals display "incarnating wisdom." Here, potential becomes realized for individuals and their community.

Incarnating wisdom means "putting flesh" on the things one knows for the sake of others. This may lead some to work at community development. It may lead others to activism and protest. For some, it means feeding the hungry by sharing one's cultural knowledge of cooking because "if the people themselves do not have a critical role in the liberation process, in the end they remain objects" (Kirylo & Boyd, 2017, p. 14). The very creation of Padres Unidos is an example of incarnating wisdom, as Patricia Huerta, the founder of the organization, used her understanding of the community to create a structure which could help others thrive. Whether the call to enflesh community knowledge in one's own life comes from the community itself or from God, the impetus to action arises from something greater than oneself. This living out process of the organic intellectual may take many forms, but essentially includes clearly articulated and enacted understandings of community knowledge and values actively put to the service of the community itself.

LET'S CHAT
CAFECITO II (Individual or Dialogue)

An organic intellectual is someone who works with the community and speaks on behalf of the community. They are also referred to as community heroes.

Who are the community (often unsung) heroes in your life?

According to your community, what makes them community heroes?

What are their extraordinary accomplishments?

Do people acknowledge their work? Why or why not?

What can we do to show them we recognize their contributions?

Activity

Gather people in your class/neighborhood/community and identify and identify, by making a list, the community heroes/organic intellectuals. What can you and your friends do to acknowledge your local heroes?

References

Butler, J. E. (2006). African american literature and realist theory In L. Alcoff, M. Hames-García, S. Mohanty, M. Hames-García & P. M. L. Moya (Eds.), *Identity politics reconsidered* (pp. 171-192). New York, NY: Palgrave Macmillan US.

Kirylo, J. D., & Boyd, D. (2017). *Paulo Freire: His faith, spirituality, and theology. Rotterdam,* The Netherlands: Sense Publishers.

Ludwig, D. (2017). The objectivity of local knowledge. Lessons from ethnobiology. *Synthese,* 194, 4705–4720. doi: 10.1007/s11229-016-1210-1

Zimmerman, A. (2017). The Role of Organic Intellectuals in the Era of a Trump Presidency. *Berkeley Review of Education.* (http://www.berkeleyreviewofeducation.com/cfc2016blog/theroleoforganicintellectualsintheeraofatrumppresidency

PRAXIS OF TOGETHERNESS

The Piano

There was a little town in Mexico whose one claim to fame was the piano that it had in the sanctuary of its church. In fact, the music of that piano was so enchanting that it brought visitors from all over the country to spend their Sunday mornings in Mass and their afternoons spending their money on the food and wares of local merchants. For a struggling little town, it was a blessing!

One day, the piano fell silent. Distressed, the parish priest, Padre Miguel, brought experts from all over the world to fix it. Not a single professional was able to repair it. Hearing the piano go silent, Gio, the custodian, knew what was wrong. When the situation had become dire, he asked the priest to let him fix the piano. Reluctantly, Padre Miguel agreed. Gio's touch brought the voice of the piano back to life. On that night he played the piano as its music filled the town, bringing with it hope to a despairing community.

Padre Miguel looked at Gio in astonishment. "All this time, I thought that I knew best about how to bring happiness and goodness to the people of this town. But tonight you have done more than I ever could. I should not take the pulpit anymore." Padre Miguel took off the priestly stole that was hanging on his shoulders and started to place it on Gio. "Clearly, you should lead this parish. You were able to fix this piano because you share the heart of the people who needed its music. I am too detached."

Gio stopped the priest. "No, Padre! We need you. You have helped this town through preaching, the sacraments, and your example. I could never do that for these people. Only a priest can. But I do realize that I have much to offer this town as a member of this community. By giving me a chance to fix this piano you showed me that." The two went on talking for hours.

The piano continues to play in the town. Its music brought Gio and Padre Miguel to see each other's gifts as well as their own. That was its blessing. Today, Padre Miguel and Gio work together on festivals, sermons, concerts, and community events. Each of them brings his own wisdom to the table, bringing all the parts of community to work together like one beautiful melodious song!

LET'S CHAT
CAFECITO I (Individual or Dialogue)

The relationship between the priest and the custodian changed in the course of the telling of the piano story. How would you describe each stage of relationship? What might the next stage look like?	Is there a time when you combined your talents and gifts with those of another for the sake of a positive outcome? What kind of relationship did you need to have in order to make such a partnership work?

Discussion

In our third telling of the piano story, we want to invite our readers to ask what new lesson is born out of this narrative when we follow Gio and Padre Miguel beyond the event of fixing the piano. More than being a story of different people coming together, this is a story of the embracing of togetherness. Before it broke, the piano would draw people together for Mass by transforming a space with its music. While they shared a memory, they did not share anything deeper. Yet, the kind of togetherness that happens with Padre Miguel and Gio is both life-changing and paradigm-shifting. It meant that they acted in the world in a new way, valuing each other and making new things happen together. This is the possibility of truly deep relationships.

Relationships are also integral to community and university partnerships. While collaborative researchers speak readily about relationship as an aspect of partnership, it is equally true that the meaning of relationship can vary greatly, depending on one's ethics and positionality. Likewise, we might expect that there is deep variance in the understanding of relationship between communities and universities in general. Considering research relationships as existing on a continuum from more to less involved, Saltmarsh and Hartley (2011) argue that deeper, more democratic relationships facilitate more profound partnerships. They explain that less engaged relationships tend to focus too narrowly and dispassionately on the minutia of a partnership rather than considering how these details relate more broadly on the purpose deepening the relationship. Shallow relationships, therefore, tend to make the university's position, interests, and motivations appear more valuable than the community's position. It is for this reason that Chapman University and Padres Unidos partners committed to a relationship which was democratic and equitable.

It is not sufficient to examine the quality of a relationship alone. In an earlier chapter, we discussed the importance of a relational ethic, one which is informed by a sense of justice, equity, and good action. The question that remains is to understand the *place* of relationships in a research partnership. Very often, we find that fellow university researchers outside of our partnership affirm that relationships are central to the community work they do. What becomes clear is that relationships are often seen as a means to an end in the research partnership. These relationships may be highly ethical and authentic. However, they remain only a facilitating aspect in the partnership geared towards a particular goal. We propose that all this ought to be profoundly shifted by making the relationship coterminous with the research goal. Its centrality is not methodological but essential. Relationship is the process *and* the goal of the partnership in every aspect.

To better understand our relationship, Padres Unidos and Chapman University partners sought to theorize what deeply ethical and relational partnerships could look like. We sought to understand our relationship by looking at theories like social ecology. This approach conjures an image of society as an interconnected web of mutually dependent organisms to which none is more indispensable than the other (Bookchin, 2005). Therefore, within the social ecology frame, ideas such as relationships take on a drastically different image than they do in other organic metaphors such as a Social Darwin model. The imagery of Darwinism often runs counter to values such as democracy or equality as they support a "survival of the fittest" attitude where, by contrast, the social ecology model shows that survival is ever-dependent on the other. The mutual dependence and reverence for the other recalls ethics philosopher Martin Buber (1970). His concept of the *I/thou* relationship insists that the *other* is an essential and existential piece of the human being. Therefore, what it means to be in partnership in this context necessarily demands that the *other* must be considered as the dialectical complement to the *self*. This means more than simply coming together, sharing moments on a weekly schedule, or co-writing a book. It means letting our togetherness inform all these actions as well as our sense of collective self.

Our partnership has been dedicated to bringing about and enacting good in our world. Thus, we are aware of Paulo Freire's (1970) warning that disembodied theories rarely have liberatory effects for those who are under the weight of oppression. Rather, he says that theorizing the world should be connected to action within that same world. He calls this praxis. It is the constant cycle of acting and understanding in which theory arises from doing, thus creating a new theory which, in turn, directs future doing. If we have made togetherness the source and summit of our *theories*, then it must likewise be the heart of our *actions*. Being together in this way means engaging in the *praxis of togetherness*. Freire intimates the centrality of relationships of this kind when he wrote: "True solidarity is found only in the plenitude of this act of love, in its existentiality, in its praxis" (Friere, 1970, p. 50). In other words, to understand the most profound relationships (solidarity), one must engage in this flow of reflection and action.

As partners, we came to this Padres-Chapman relationship as organic intellectuals and scholarly activists. We lived the relationship first by embracing the practice of epistemological modesty and incarnating wisdom, each according to their positionality. Through the years we have learned a great deal by relating and understanding our relationship in this continuous reflexive cycle. The *praxis of togetherness* enacts a vulnerability, one which is open to "You" and "I" being transformed into a radically inclusive "We." SooHoo (2016) contextualized the practice of this vulnerability in a Frierean frame when she wrote, "we must offer our mutual unfinishedness as the foundation for our co-constructed agenda" (p. xi). When we come to relate as unfinished beings in this partnership, we find that living out this praxis has concrete consequences. In our research conversations, we have discovered that there are some ideas that are only accessible to us as partners *when we are together*. That is, in our meetings we arrive at new knowledge, but trying to understand that same idea separately from the collective moments of togetherness has proven impossible. We write and present together, not simply for moral support, but because all that we know and have become in this partnership is inextricably intertwined to the relationality we share. This is an interdependence of knowledge. It answers a question that Suzanne SooHoo often asks students in her classes: What can we know together that we could never have known apart? We are engaging the untested feasibility of togetherness as we commit to ethical and equitable relationship (Freire, 2002). Because, as community and university partners, we are all individuals constantly involved in the process of becoming more human and engaged in the dynamic praxis of togetherness; our knowledge and relationship is likewise unfinished. It is directed forward by hope.

As a community of knowers in relationship, we have committed to share with you what we are coming to know together. We have grown in our work, sensed transformation, given birth to new knowledge, embraced challenge, troubled old paradigms, and written about new concepts. All this has come to be because we have first and continually engaged in our togetherness. To the extent that this relationship is authentic, these realities are authentic. We invite you to consider engaging in partnerships which do not simply utilize relationship but which ultimately *are* relationship. It all starts with an encounter with others. A handshake or a greeting with no ulterior motive to achieve something other than the possibility of togetherness. We put before you our own partnership as evidence that untold possibilities may unfold from there.

LET'S CHAT
CAFECITO II (Individual or Dialogue)

What would you do if you were in a partnership relationship and you were asked to make a presentation that only one person could present? Who would make the presentation? How would you make the decision? How would a relational ethic inform your choices?

Activity

Co-author a short publication with at least five people. What are the different criteria from which you could use to order authorship that acknowledges equal value to different aspects of participation? How could you make the decision?

Ideally, given the constraints of two-dimensional linearity, we wish we could list authorship to indicate equality: Stockbridge=Meza=Bolin=Huerta=SooHoo. Unfortunately, we've tried this approach. The Library of Congress would not allow it.

References

Bookchin, M. (2005). *The ecology of freedom: The emergence and dissolution of hierarchy.* Oakland, CA: AK Press.

Buber, M. (1970). *I and thou.* New York, NY: Charles Scribner's Sons.

Freire, P. (1970). *Pedagogy of the oppressed.* NY: Continuum.

Freire, P. (2002). *Pedagogy of hope.* New York, NY: Continuum.

Saltmarsh, J. & Hartley, M. (Eds). (2011). *To serve a larger purpose: Engagement for democracy and the transformation of higher education.* Philadelphia: Temple University Press.

SooHoo. (2016). Foreword: Double consciousness for all. In Hartlep, N.D. & Hayes, C. (Eds.) *Unhooking from whiteness: Resisting the Esprit de Corps.* (pp. ix-xii). Boston, MA: Sense Publishers.

Scope & Sequence

SECTION 1	Coming to Know	Topic	Activity	Outcome
	Chapter 1	Partnership	Craft a step-by-step plan on how you would build relationships with those whom you wish to engage. Include community protocols you would observe	Planning protocol for community engagement
	Chapter 2	Togethering	Set up a time to have a shared meal. Consider rituals that allow for and/or hinder togethering	Engaging in community
	Chapter 3	Knowledge	Share your favorite memory of something that you learned in school with a friend. Examine the conditions and context of that memory to determine what made it a good learning experience	Building cultural knowledge

SECTION 2	Becoming	Topic	Activity	Outcome
	Chapter 4	Walking With	Learning Walk	Embodying the learning process
	Chapter 5	Communal Structures	Conduct a mini-ethnography and study the way your organization operates	Review the organizational plan
	Chapter 6	Dialogue and Cultural Circles	Present and compare two mini-presentations on the same topic – one that is designed as a lecture and one that is designed for people to engage in dialogue cultural circles	Enact a cultural circle
	Chapter 7	Teaching and Learning	Use the *Padres Unidos* problem-posing/problem-solving questions in one of your small group conversations	Consider an inclusive, dialogical curriculum for teaching and learning
	Chapter 8	Resiliency	Design a resiliency and resourcefulness plan	Articulate a strategic plan for implementation

	Belonging	Topic	Activity	Outcome
SECTION 3	Chapter 9	Spirituality	Imagine that someone is writing about the unique qualities of your family or group	Conceptualize insider/outsider status
	Chapter 10	Ethics and Democracy	Make a list of the core values (ethical/moral principles) that inform and hold true in your club or organizations	Articulate core values
	Chapter 11	Transformation and Hope	Develop three good questions that would help your organization conduct a reflective assessment of its strengths and weaknesses	Create a reflection tool
	Chapter 12	Scholarly Activist	Conduct a self-inventory of what knowledge, skills, talents and experiences you bring to the community	Perform a self-assessment
	Chapter 13	Organic Intellectual	With your class or community, identify and make a list of community heroes/organic intellectuals	Recognize community heroes
	Chapter 14	Praxis of Togetherness	Co-author a short publication with at least five people	Memorialize a history of work

About the Authors

Researchers from the Paulo Freire Democratic Project at Chapman University – Suzanne SooHoo, Tim Bolin and Kevin Stockbridge – and Padres Unidos' organizational leaders – Patricia Huerta and Patty Perales Huerta-Meza – cocreated this book based on a partnership that began in 2010. It features what they learned from each other, as well as what they hope, through this book, will contribute to the learning of others.

About the Design Team

"SooHoo", whose business is engaging people by design – is proud and privileged to have been an integral part of contributing to this unique "coffee table textbook." The team of Patrick SooHoo, Kathy Hirata, Atilio Rugamas, Cheryl Kubo, Katie Low and especially the talents of Cindy Hahn – created illustrations and layouts into the midnight hours to achieve the notable aesthetics and accessibility.